THE POETRY OF FAITH

THE POETRY OF FAITH

Sermons Preached in a Southern Church

STEPHEN F. DILL

EDITED AND WITH AN INTRODUCTION BY
FRYE GAILLARD

NEWSOUTH BOOKS

Montgomery

NewSouth Books
105 S. Court Street
Montgomery, AL 36104

ISBN 978-1-60306-278-7 (paperback)
ISBN 978-1-60306-279-4 (ebook)

Design by Randall Williams
Photo on page ii by Allen Oaks

Printed in the United States of America
by Versa Press

For Ruth—

and those she gave me!

Contents

Introduction

The first time I ever heard a Steve Dill sermon, he was preaching in an African-American church. It was Emancipation Day in 2005, a joyous occasion celebrating the New Year's morning in 1863 when Abraham Lincoln issued the Emancipation Proclamation. In September of 1862, President Lincoln had delivered a preliminary declaration, promising freedom on New Year's Day, and it was said that slaves and abolitionists all over the country gathered in churches to await the final word.

In the Methodist church, these "Watch Night" services dovetailed with an even older tradition—John Wesley's introduction in 1740 of a prayerful alternative to the raucous revelries of New Year's Eve. For Steve Dill, whose sermons are collected in this book, Watch Night was a deeply meaningful occasion. He had long admired the historic leadership of John Wesley, and he admired also the traditions of the African-American church.

As a young minister in Montgomery in the 1960s, he had confronted head-on the issues of racism and civil rights. One of the members of his church in those days was a man by the name of C. H. Lancaster, a leader in the White Citizens Council. In 1965, shortly after the Selma to Montgomery march, Lancaster led an unsuccessful effort to exclude African-Americans from Sunday morning worship at the church.

On April 11, 1965, in a statement he read to the congregation, Lancaster framed the issue this way: "The present controversy raging within the Dalraida Methodist Church is over the basic question: Shall we remain a White Christian church or a Racially Mixed body?"

"I do not intend," he continued, "to remain in any service while a member of the African race is present. . . . They come not to worship but to mock. They are part and parcel of the immoral mob aided by the National Council of Churches that staged the infamous march from Selma to Montgomery. As for me, I will not suffer my wife and children to sit amongst them."

Steve Dill did his best to stay calm. Then as now, he knew the theological issues were clear, and quietly he set about persuading the church's lay leadership that he was right. From the vantage point of more than forty years later, the whole controversy can seem surreal. Was it really possible that Methodists in Montgomery, or anywhere else, would seriously question the brotherhood of man? Would they actually argue that skin color determined the fitness for worship? That was precisely what was happening, and emotions on the issue were running high. When the board of directors at Dalraida Methodist sustained Dill's view that worship must be open to anyone, regardless of race, Lancaster called it a "craven acquiescence" and withdrew from the church.

Looking back on the times, Gorman Houston, a former United Methodist minister and a friend and protégé of Dill's, said the two of them talked often about social issues. "They were huge for Steve," said Houston. "I heard him talk about how in those civil rights days, they lived with the issue every day. But he was on the right side of history and he knew it. Basically, it came down to an absolute assurance that he and others had that they were right. It gave them courage. Steve was one of those ministers who were able to see the church as it should be and not as it was."

But in Houston's view, there was more to the story than that. "Steve never lost himself in the battle," he said. "That was what was so remarkable to me. He never distanced himself from the people he disagreed with. He had a pastoral way, never letting go of his strong stands, but also never letting go of his kindness. I remember Steve saying about a person others might regard as a bigot, 'He just has a blind spot on the race issue.' That goes to the heart of who Steve is."

Houston first came to know Dill well when they served together at Dauphin Way United Methodist Church in Mobile. Dill became the senior minister at the church in 1972, a position he held until 1990. Houston was an associate minister for three of those years, and a few years after Dill's retirement, when Houston became senior minister himself, he was delighted that Steve and his wife, Ruth, had remained as active members of the church. "It was like having your parents in the pew," he said.

For both Houston and Dill, there was always something a little daunting about Dauphin Way. It seemed to be filled with the shadow and the spirit of one of the great preachers of the twentieth century. Carl Adkins, a native of Kentucky, had come to the church in 1941, and Dauphin Way, under his leadership, continued an impressive evolution from its log cabin origins of 1913. For one thing, its new sanctuary offered such a beautiful place to worship, with its stained-glass windows and mahogany pews, and on most Sunday mornings the soaring music of the choir. And there was also the pulpit presence of Adkins, who served the church until his death from cancer in 1966. He was always such an eloquent speaker, and he brought in guest ministers who were equally as gifted, and that became the identity of Dauphin Way. It was a place where the Sunday morning message took on a kind of poetry and force, and after Adkins' death, the baton was passed to Joel McDavid, who served until 1972.

Then came Steve Dill, who set out to build on a legacy he already knew was important—an understanding of the Christian message as a powerful inter-weaving of mystery and truth, an anchor and a guide for daily living, but never a reason to be complacent or smug; to end the search for deeper understanding. In delivering that message, Dill was more understated in the pulpit than Adkins was, but in Houston's mind he was no less impressive.

"Steve had such a presence," Houston said, "as if he were made for that pulpit at Dauphin Way. He was the right height, the right bearing. When he was preaching, he was preaching to dear friends that he loved and cared for. His sermons were rational, reasonable; the theological depth would always be present. You never had to worry if it would be trite or simplistic, and he would open our minds to whatever social issues were at hand. There were some people who were not as into theology and who sometimes thought of Steve's sermons as being too hard to digest. 'It seems like God talking, but I don't understand what he is saying.' You'd hear people say things like that. But even for those people it **sounded** so good. There was a comfort in just being there to hear it."

In Dill's own estimation, he encountered an unexpected chance to improve on his preaching during a particularly difficult time for Dauphin Way. Gorman Houston, who, after Dill's retirement, had become perhaps his most beloved successor, decided in 2010 to leave the ministry and accept a teaching job at the University of Alabama. To the congregation, the move seemed sudden, and the members were reeling with a sense of loss, when Dill agreed to be their interim minister. Even he will admit (and he can be a stiff and unrelenting critic) that he probably did his best preaching during that time, which is not at all hard for me to believe. I first heard him during those months, preaching, for example, on an Easter morning about the history of the Resurrection story. He quoted Frederick Buechner about how we in the western world, burdened with our rational, scientific minds, can buttress the leap of faith required to believe in something so literally implausible as a dead man walking. We want to believe, and our Sunday school certainties tell us that we should; and yet many of us, if we are honest, are shadowed by the doubts of our rational minds. Buechner, the great American theologian and novelist, proclaimed that essentially it comes down to this: "all we need to know that somehow he got up with the life in him and glory upon him and the world is flooded with light."

Steve Dill picked up the story from there, arguing for those still inclined to doubt that **something** happened in the history of those times—something so remarkable and dramatic that it transformed a beaten-down band of disciples into confident proclaimers of the Christian faith. And of course that was true. A group of followers that was small to begin with, and devastated by the horrors of the crucifixion, suddenly began to preach with such force that they transformed the spiritual history of the world. The point was obvious when I thought about it, but oddly enough I never had—at least not exactly in that way—and I discovered that was often the case with Steve Dill sermons.

Almost invariably, the poetry of his preaching caught the quick of my imagination and quietly, inevitably made me think. I began to talk about this with other friends in the church—with Kimi Oaks and Jim and Becky Bell—and this is what they said in reply.

"We were enriched by his sermons and his leadership of Dauphin Way," said Kimi. "Still today, with his shock of white hair and ramrod straight carriage, Steve stands tall amongst us, bearing an image of wisdom and inspiring both confidence and trust. There is a softness about Steve, but always a steely commitment to the cause of Christ . . ."

And Becky Bell added, "His sermons were like a salve to our souls. . . ."

My wife, Nancy, was the first to suggest, about this time, that we put together this volume of reflections. The timing of it seemed to be right. The year 2013 would mark the hundredth anniversary of Dauphin Way, and the book could be a part of that celebration. But we believed also that the wisdom contained in Steve Dill's sermons could have a broader application, a view that was shared emphatically by Jeff and Robin Wilson, the new senior ministers at Dauphin Way.

They both remembered their first meeting with the Dills, with Steve and his wife, Ruth, always a critical part of his ministry. "We had never met Steve and Ruth before coming here," said Jeff. "I knew they had served for a long time and were deeply respected in the church. Our first encounter with Steve came at a lunch, and he was gracious and warm and hospitable, so encouraging and available to Robin and me. He made it clear that he was there to support us."

"He and Ruth could have been checking us out," said Robin. "Instead, they made us feel like we were coming home."

And so we have put together this book, this collection of sermons that reflect what Robin called "the bold humility" of Steve Dill's ministry. Steve worked with us, reluctantly at first, wondering aloud about whether he had said anything worth preserving. But we managed to persuade him to go through his files and to pull together what is, in a sense, a journey of reflection, spanning a full year on the Christian calendar.

Happily for me, the book begins with the first of Dill's sermons that I had ever heard, that Emancipation Day message delivered on January 1, 2005. Steve had been asked by his African-American hosts to offer the Christian apology for slavery, one of the most daunting assignments I could imagine. He selected as his Biblical text that morning a passage from Galatians: **all of you are one in Christ Jesus**. But he chose another text as well, a phrase he repeated throughout the sermon as he quoted from his favorite Negro spiritual: **Were you there when they crucified my Lord? / Sometimes it causes me to tremble. . . .**

The poetry of this particular sermon was something that I never forgot, and it sets the tone, I think, for everything that follows in this book. Our hope for those of you who read these words is that you will be as moved to the same contemplations that we are. In saying this, I speak as a skeptic, as one afflicted periodically by the shadow of doubt, but even more as a reluctant critic of American Christianity—of the didactic shrillness emanating from so many of our pulpits—a reality that, for me at least, often gives the faith a bad name.

You won't find any of that from Steve Dill, nothing harsh, or narrow, or petty; nothing simplistic or disingenuous. Instead, what you'll discover, I think, is a rigorous mind in search of deeper truth, and a faith in the loving mysteries of God. You'll also find the same six words at the end of every sermon, offered, quite clearly, not to exclude anyone of another faith, but as a humble affirmation of his own:

In the name of Christ, Amen.

FRYE GAILLARD

Writer in Residence
University of South Alabama

THE POETRY OF FAITH

1.

It Causes Me to Tremble

y good friend, the Reverend Dr. Wesley A. James, pastor of Franklin Street Missionary Baptist Church and a strong civic leader, called me one day on behalf of the Mobile Baptist Sunlight Association. He asked if I would speak at the annual Service of Emancipation to be held January 1, 2005, at the historic Stewart Memorial Christian Methodist Episcopal Church in Mobile.

President Abraham Lincoln issued the Emancipation Proclamation on January 1, 1863. The night before, Americans of African descent gathered in churches to await the news that the president would indeed sign the Proclamation of Freedom. Afterwards, black Americans developed a tradition of returning to church on New Year's Eve or New Year's Day to commemorate the end of slavery.

Dr. James asked me to speak at the Service of Emancipation and offer a Christian apology for slavery. It was a daunting assignment and yet a satisfying one. As a Southern Christian, I had long felt pained over the institution of slavery and its lasting effect. It was important to me to formulate my thoughts and to worship with these, my brothers and sisters, in this historic service. My remarks were entitled, "It Causes Me to Tremble":

> *By this everyone will know that you are my disciples, if you have love for one another.*
>
> JOHN 13:35 (NIV)

> *For all of you as were baptized into Christ have clothed yourselves with Christ. There is no longer Jew or Greek, there is no longer slave or free, there is no longer male and female; for all of you are one in Christ Jesus.*
>
> GALATIANS 3:27–28 (NIV)

3

FIRST LET ME WISH you a happy and prosperous New Year and ask that you pray that 2005 brings peace to our troubled world. We must also pray for all those people along the Indian Ocean rim who have suffered such tragedy in the recent tsunami.

It is a joy to be with you and to see so many with whom I have worked throughout the years. It is a privilege to be present on this historic occasion in this historic church. One hundred forty-two years ago, in the midst of the Civil War, Abraham Lincoln signed the Emancipation Proclamation, which has undoubtedly shaped the destiny of our nation.

Today, I am called upon to apologize to the African-American community for the white citizens' participation in the institution of slavery. The task overwhelms me! I cannot comprehend the extent of the suffering, the humiliation, the constraint of hope, and the extensive cultural damage caused by that inhumanity. In the eighteenth century, John Wesley called it "the sum of all villainies," and American slavery "the vilest under the sun."[1]

Slavery is the kind of life described by poet Paul Laurence Dunbar:

> A crust of bread and a corner to sleep in,
> A minute to smile and an hour to weep in,
> A pint of joy to a peck of trouble,
> And never a laugh, but the moans come double:
> And that is life![2]

Many would like to say that American slavery was over and done with when Lincoln signed the Emancipation Proclamation, but slavery's restrictive shadow falls across our nation still. As William Faulkner said, "The past is not dead. In fact, it is not even past."[3]

Apologize? What could one apology possibly mean? I was not alive all those years ago when the Emancipation Proclamation was signed. Nor can I apologize for another person; I cannot read another person's heart nor see into another person's soul. And yet, though I was not alive when American slavery was enforced, I can recognize the tragic aftermath of slavery on our culture and on our people, both black and white. I have seen the separate and *un*-equal education, the *partial* justice, and the demeaning poverty that in large measure resulted from that horrific practice.

So let me begin with this. My Christian faith and the Christian faith of the African-American community have guided me in this overwhelming task of framing an apology. Even though slavery existed before our time, Christians can easily understand the nature and the necessity of reconciliation. Just because the crucifixion of Christ occurred before my time, long before I was born, does that mean that I am uninvolved? The black community helps me understand my part in the suffering of Christ when it sings, "Were you there when they crucified my Lord? / Were you there when they nailed Him to the tree? / Were you there when they laid Him in the tomb? / Oh, sometimes, it causes me to tremble . . . tremble . . . tremble!"

I believe my sin helped to place Him on the Cross; I believe He died for me! It happened before I was born, but still, I trust the benefits of His passion for my salvation. This Christian faith is such an amazing grace; it o'er-leaps time to bring me my redemption. In the same way, can it not be true in some appropriate degree, that my prejudice today, my greed, my thoughtlessness, my hostility, must be considered in the crushing weight of slavery? Were you there? Was I there, when men and women were bought and sold? Was I there when slavery separated family members from one another? Was I there when humanity lost all regard for its fellow creature? "Oh, sometimes it causes me to tremble!"

I have labored throughout my ministry to foster understanding between the races, to cross the cultural and denominational divides, to move beyond the boundaries of prejudice, bigotry, and discrimination. And yet, I am compelled to recognize my slowness in feeling another's pain, my hesitancy in challenging the unfair systems. I am compelled to recognize my comfortable position, so often insensible and insulated from my neighbor's distress.

As I look back across more than fifty years of ministry, the painful moments are all too real and relevant—segregation of the schools and churches, failure to use the titles of respect, the unfair systems of economy and law. But still, I relish in some magnificent moments of reconciliation—of darkness being overcome by light—occasions of friendship and grace, small things, seemingly unimportant things, which took on God's meaning. For:

When I am with God all life has meaning.
Big things become small and small things become great.
The near becomes far and the future is near.
The lowly and despised are shot through with glory.[4]

I remember a Brotherhood Service with Dr. Joseph Lowery fifty years ago. During the service a young woman, without announcement, quietly stepped into the aisle. She stood there with her hand on the back of the pew, not facing the congregation. With a magnificent voice and obvious conviction, she sang, "Talk about a child that do love Jesus, here's one, here's one. / Talk about a child who's been converted, here's one. / Ever since I heard the gospel story, I've been walking up the path to glory. / Talk about a child that do love Jesus, here's one."[5] It touched me so deeply; I remember it as if it were yesterday.

I remember little things, funny things! Many years ago, I directed a church camp for junior high students at Blue Lake Assembly Grounds. One delegation was black; one group of white young people was snobbish and unfriendly. The Youth Council was concerned, and they discussed at great length how they might lead in demonstrating friendship. Finally, a lovely black girl who was a member of the council gave them a simple solution. She said, "Just smile. It ain't no big deal."

In Celebration 2000, the Christian community of Mobile commemorated two thousand years of faith. There were many brilliant moments. Christians representing a diversity of churches and institutions gathered from across the community to celebrate two thousand years of Christian love and grace. The planning and the program were varied and inclusive. I had hoped it was a new beginning for a new century. I could envision Christians with renewed dedication, enriched by new friendships and mutual respect, talking together, praying together, learning together, worshiping together, working together.

But, so far as I can see, there was little lasting effect, and it troubles me that we are not further along the way. In a more subtle form, the same separation, prejudice, and evil are present today as in the time of slavery. It is a never-ending battle. The Christian community must create the channels of communication until reconciliation is real. Christians have too often been thermometers instead of thermostats. Too often we have simply registered the surrounding temperature: Where there was criticism, we became critical; where there was prejudice, we accepted the culture of injustice. Christians have not often enough controlled the temperature; we have not changed the climate. "Sometimes, it causes me to tremble!"

My ministry goes back a long way, and throughout the years I have been troubled by the frequent lack of Christian charity, troubled by the separateness and hatred between the races, troubled by the prejudice and the conformity I have witnessed and endured. My joy in being here today is not because it is comfortable, but because it is cleansing. Being here is not without anxiety and regret, but it is healing and redemptive.

So what *did* motivate me to be present today? Basically, I am here because Jesus said, **"By this all men will know that you are my disciples, if you have love for one another."** (John 13:35) I believe we are here together, because Saint Paul said, **"For many of you as were baptized into Christ have clothed yourselves with Christ. There is no longer Jew or Greek, there is no longer slave or free, there is no longer male and female; for all are one in Jesus Christ."** (Galatians 3:27,28) Thanks be to God that many of us are here because friendship and Christian grace have been offered across the barriers of culture, denomination, tradition, and race.

So, if there is to be any reconciliation, it must begin with the churches. We must learn to be deliberately inclusive, inviting other Christians into our circles of prayer and praise and Bible study. The Church must cross the lines of denomination and race in worship, hearing other Christians teach and preach, pray and sing. What a force the churches could be, laboring together in compassionate efforts to bring health and healing to a sick and troubled world!

You have already come a long way. I stand in awe of those black leaders who, across the world, have answered violence with nonviolence and injury with forgiveness. I went back and read the speeches of Dr. Martin Luther King, Jr., and without exception, from the beginning of the bus boycott, to the march on Washington, to the Nobel Prize, he consistently held to the position of nonviolence.

At the funeral for four little girls killed in the bombing at Sixteenth

Street Baptist Church in Birmingham, he said, "So in spite of the darkness of this hour we must not despair. We must not become bitter; nor must we harbor the desire to retaliate with violence. We must not lose faith in our white brothers. Somehow we must believe that the most misguided among them can learn to respect the dignity and worth of all human personality."[6]

I think not only of national leaders but also of those closer to home, like Thomas Gilmore, the first black sheriff of Greene County, Alabama, who never carried a gun. Or I remember the great multitude of citizens in the South who suffered the discrimination of race and refused to hate. "Through many dangers, toils, and snares, you have already come," and through it all you have pointed the way to reconciliation. "Sometimes, it causes me to tremble!"

When Nelson Mandela, after twenty-seven years in prison, was elected president of South Africa, he said, "From the moment the results were in and it was apparent that the ANC (African National Congress) was to form the government, I saw my mission as one of preaching reconciliation, of binding the wounds of the country, of engendering trust and confidence."[7]

On May 8, 1994, in South Africa, where President Mandela and the Christian leadership had successfully avoided a blood bath, a National Service of Thanksgiving was held. Included in the service was an Act of Reconciliation and Sharing of the Peace. It was not judgmental or one-sided. It was a beautiful moment. Together, they said, "We struggled against one another: now we are reconciled to struggle for one another. We believed it was right to withstand one another: now we are reconciled to understand one another. We suffered a separateness that did not work: now we are reconciled to make togetherness work. We tried to frighten one another into submission: now we are reconciled to lift one another into fulfillment. We acknowledge the presence of Christ among us who reconciles the world."[8]

A Christian apology is a request for forgiveness; they are one and the same. When I have sinned and ask forgiveness for my callousness, my lack of sensitivity, my unwillingness to forgive, the Heavenly Father requires me to seek out the injured party, if that is possible, and ask for forgiveness. And after that, I am obligated to do everything in my power to repair the damage, to change the climate, to prevent any recurrence of injury, and to build a new relationship.

The hour is late, but with God, it is not *too late*. I can think of many who have repented late of their bigoted position. There may be some here who lately have come to an awareness that they must be forgiven and be involved in redemptive work. Saint Augustine begins a prayer, "Late have I loved thee, O Beauty so ancient and so new; late have I loved thee: for behold thou wert within me, and I outside. . . . Thou wert with me, and I was not with thee." It may be late, but it is never *too late*. There is much that we can do. We can ask for forgiveness. We can forgive when we are asked. We can do everything in our power to change the climate so that brotherhood and peace abound.

I was so impressed with little Nkosi Johnson, who had been South Africa's longest surviving child born HIV-positive. He died at age twelve, weighing less than twenty-two pounds. But in July 2000, this slight child with the soulful eyes and full-blown AIDS captured the heart of millions of viewers when his address to the 13th International AIDS Conference in Durban, South Africa,[9] was televised worldwide. He said, "Care for us and accept us; we are all human beings. We are normal. We have hands, we have feet, we can walk, we can talk. We have needs just like everyone else. Don't be afraid of us; we are all the same."

Nkosi was bright, courageous, and he possessed wisdom beyond his years. We would do well to heed his simple and direct advice. This was the decree he lived by; he said, "Do all you can, with what you have, in the time you have, in the place you are."

Now, because of all these things, I do not hesitate to ask for your forgiveness, and I pray that others in our community and across the world will join with us, until it is accepted and commonplace, that we are "all one in Christ Jesus." Our separation has been too long, O Lord, too long. And sometimes, it causes me to tremble.

In the name of Christ, *Amen.*

Notes

1   Wesley, John, "Thoughts Upon Slavery," pamphlet, and a letter to William Wilberforce; texts at the United Methodist Global Ministries website.

2   Dunbar, Paul Laurence, "Life."

3   Faulkner, William, *Requiem for a Nun,* Act 1, Scene 3.

4   Rauschenbusch, Walter, "The Little Gate to God."

5   Dawson, William L., "Talk About a Child."

6   Carson, Clayborne, *The Autobiography of Martin Luther King, Jr.,* Warner Books, 1998, p. 232.

7   Mandela, Nelson, *Long Walk to Freedom*, Little, Brown, 1994, p. 619.

8   Tutu, Desmond, *An African Prayer Book*, Doubleday, 1995, p. 40.

9   Johnson, Nkosi, address to 13th International AIDS Conference.

2.

The Power of His Compliment

In 2013 the congregation of Dauphin Way United Methodist Church marks its one hundredth year of serving its Master and witnessing to the Lordship of Jesus Christ. It is important for the visible Church to remember what it means to be the Church and to count the cost of tomorrow's discipleship. In the months leading up to the Centennial Celebration, I preached on "The Power of His Compliment":

> *A dispute also arose among them as to which one of them was to be regarded as the greatest. But he said to them, "The kings of the Gentiles lord it over them; and those in authority over them are called benefactors. But not so with you; rather the greatest among you must become like the youngest, and the leader like one who serves. For who is greater, the one who is at the table or the one who serves? Is it not the one at the table? But I am among you as one who serves. You are those who have stood by me in my trials; and I confer on you, just as my Father has conferred on me, a kingdom, so that you may eat and drink at my table in my kingdom, and you will sit on thrones judging the twelve tribes of Israel."*
>
> LUKE 22:24–30 (NIV)

THERE WERE SO MANY times when Jesus was disappointed by His disciples, in today's lesson for example. It is the Last Supper, the mood is somber, the crisis impending. Jesus is facing the end of His earthly ministry, and, of all things, a jealous dispute breaks out among the disciples over who should be ranked the highest. Just an instant before, they were shocked to learn that one of them would betray Jesus, and now there is an argument over which of them is the greatest. Surprisingly, at this moment Jesus offers them an unforgettable compliment! He says to them: **"You are the ones who have stood by me through my trials."**

The truth is, they were not much for which to be grateful. They continually failed to understand him. He said to Philip, **"Have I been with you all this time and you still don't know me?"** Judas would betray him; Peter would deny him; even at the moment of his compliment they were contending over rank and status. About all you could say for them was that they were there; they had not given up.

And actually, that was no small thing. These difficult years were not what they had expected. The popularity of Jesus had faded, His opposition had mounted, and the illusive Kingdom of God had failed to appear. At that very moment there were many dangers: Judas had already slipped out to bring the soldiers to arrest Jesus. But, at least they had not quit, and Jesus was clearly grateful. Without a doubt, He needed them! We must not forget His humanity, "the word was made flesh." Just as we all do, He needed the encouragement and understanding of faithful friends. And, in gratitude for their friendship, He offered them a sincere compliment.

And what a compliment it was! **"You are those who have stood by me through my trials. And just as surely as my Father has assigned to me a Kingdom, I assign a Kingdom to you, to eat and drink at my table, to sit on thrones and judge the twelve tribes of Israel."** That must have been an unforgettable moment, a compliment that stuck in their minds and hearts giving them courage and keeping them loyal until the very end.

Now, here we are as a congregation, approaching one hundred years of service and facing the future as committed disciples. In 2013, Dauphin Way will celebrate its Centennial. We have been together as a congregation for almost ten decades, but that, of course, is only a brief moment in the history of Christendom. Still, no charter member of the church remains; it is a new congregation, with new leadership—or today you might say *"old* leadership!" We are facing new challenges, being given new opportunities. The record thus far is creditable, but certainly not faultless. With deeper commitment and greater wisdom we could have, should have, accomplished more for Christ. Yet, we were here, on His side, counting for something, being faithful!

And what of the future? Will we be faithful in the future? What, I wonder, awaits us as we attempt to follow the Master? Will the years bring hardship and humiliation or will the ship of Christ sail on calm and tranquil seas? Whatever the future brings, it won't be the same, and it won't be what we expect. The congregation changes, the world changes, the leadership changes, the issues are never the same. Everything changes except our commitment to Christ and His great love; that must not change. Jesus said to His disciples, **"You are the ones who have stood by me through my trials."** And if the church is to be the Church, and the grace of God is to continue to be dispensed through both faith and works, there must be disciples in this generation who stand by Him.

If we could hear Jesus offering us that compliment at this moment, it would quicken our lives and give purpose and direction to our future. Think about it! Just imagine Jesus expressing, to you personally, gratitude for standing beside Him through all the pitfalls of this present generation: the hostility and war, the greed and self-interest, the discrimination, hunger, and disease, the neglect of children, the disdain for values, all the baseness that has opposed benevolence in our time. What would be your response to hearing Christ say, "You were one of those who stood by me through all the troubles that have tested me in this current generation."

I think our first reaction would be one of humiliation. It was, I'm sure, the first reaction of the disciples. Unhappy memories flashed through their minds. James and John remembered their rebuke when Jesus said, **"You do not know what spirit you are of."** Peter recalled the Lord's censure: **"Get thee behind me, Satan."** That deplorable scene when they tried to keep the children away from Him was reenacted in their mind's eye, and they recalled how terrified they were on the Sea of Galilee. They reviewed the times their courage failed, and their faith faltered. Perhaps, in their own time, in their own way, they prayed a prayer like James Montgomery prayed:

> In the hour of trial, Jesus, plead for me;
> Lest by base denial, I depart from Thee.

When thou see'st me waver, with a look recall,
Nor for fear or favor suffer me to fall.

Yes, our reaction would be one of humiliation were we to receive such a compliment. First, we would remember those times when we were not at our best—not so wise, not so well-behaved—times when we could have done more, sacrificed more, served more, loved more.

There is a peculiar thing about most of us: let someone criticize us, and our defenses are aroused; let someone praise us, and we accuse ourselves. If some stranger were to accuse us of neglecting our children, we would rail against him for not knowing, not understanding, not minding his own business. But, let a child who is about to marry or leave for college say, "Thank you for all you have done; you have been wonderful parents to me." We would just melt, and we would protest, "Oh no, not nearly good enough parents." And all the regrettable memories would arise, of how we might have prepared them better, served them better, spent more time with them, if we had a second chance. I have seen it so often in the church. When I expressed appreciation to some of you for your generous support, the inevitable response was, "I haven't done anything, not nearly enough." Reacting to criticism, we defend ourselves; responding to gratitude, we accuse ourselves. The difference is the way we react to someone who loves us, someone who loves us and depends on us in spite of all our weaknesses. Jesus said, **"You are the ones who have stood by me through my trials."**

It would not only be a humbling experience to receive the compliment of Jesus, but it would be a clarifying one. I can imagine that compliment becoming "credentials" in the early Church—one believer asking another, "What do you believe? To whom do you give allegiance, Paul, Cephas, Apollos?" (I Cor. 1:12) And the answer would come, "We are the ones who stood by Jesus of Nazareth." After all, isn't that what gives identity to life: to know what one stands for, to know who one stands for? To see the best, even in the worst times, and to stand by that. To all appearances, to all the world, it may not make one bit of difference, but that is not the point:

You say the little efforts that I make will do no good:
They never will prevail to tip the hovering scale
Where justice hangs in balance.
I don't think I ever thought they would.
But I am prejudiced beyond debate
In favor of my right to choose which side
Shall feel the stubborn ounces of my weight.[1]

So much of our political stalemate is re-election posturing or party-protection. More and more, the thoughtful politicians tell us that they can do so little good, because the average person has no great vision, stands for nothing beyond personal aggrandizement. I am convinced whenever something worthwhile is accomplished, there you will find some unselfish service. It is certainly true in the Church; the Church reaches up toward greatness when the average member discovers a vision of the Kingdom of God and begins to be available for God's great causes.

We don't know how to measure our own self-worth. We look at things like wealth, family heritage, success, and public acclaim. But, it is really not a question of what we accomplish, for who can be the judge? Nor, should it be a question of receiving recognition, for human accolades are fleeting. But believe me, there is a tremendous, lasting satisfaction in being identified by Christ as one who stood by Him.

I wish you *could* hear Christ saying that to you! For some of you have not had much to give by the standards of this world, but you gave what you could, more than you should perhaps, regularly and faithfully. And some of you had little in the way of leadership to offer, but quietly, in your own way, you stood by and stood up for Christ. Some of you gave your energy and resources in the prolonged illness of a relative, a parent, or a child. Or you prayed for the church, or sang God's praises, or taught in the church school, or you became the door through which some other soul entered God's Kingdom of life and light. Jesus is saying to you, "You are the ones, you stood by me!"

In those critical days of the Second World War, when the outcome was still in doubt, and everything depended on production, and in England, production depended on coal, three thousand union leaders were invited to Methodist Central Hall in London to hear the Prime Minister, Winston Churchill. He spoke to them frankly and at length about the grimness of the situation. But he closed by pointing to the day when peace would come. "When the last brutal hand of tyranny had been struck down," he said, "there would be a great parade." In it would march all those who served in the great cause.

He pictured it, a great throng in Piccadilly, with Montgomery and his men sweeping past. "And what did you do?" a voice would cry from the crowd. "We fought at El Alamein." Then the men of the Royal Air Force would pass by, the few to whom the many owed so much. "And what did you do?" would come the cry. "We drove the Luftwaffe out of the sky." Then would come the men of the merchant marine who got the vital supplies to England.

Last of all, a great host of men would march by, with begrimed faces and miners lamps on their caps. "And what did you do?" would come the cry. And from ten thousand throats would come the answer, "We were deep in the pits, with our faces against the coal."[2]

Now, labor leaders are not notoriously sentimental, but at that point the whole audience rose and cheered so that Churchill could not continue. What had he done? All he had done was to let them see that they were needed in a great cause, and that their leader cared and understood.

There are probably none of us here who are great in the Kingdom of God. Yet, still He says to us, **"You are the ones who have stood by me through my trials."** What does it mean? It means we make a difference. It means we are needed, desperately needed, for the victory to be complete. It means our Lord and Leader holds us in high esteem and depends on us to do what we have been called to do.

In Galatians (5:22f) when St Paul counsels us to be guided by God's Holy Spirit, he says that among other virtues, "faithfulness" is one of the fruits of the Spirit. In this context, he is not talking about right belief or passing some creedal test. He means that a faithful person is trustworthy, dependable, one that can be relied upon. Our church has been here almost one hundred years (I have been here a long time). During that time there have been some who have fallen away, drifted away, who felt the faith was too demanding or perhaps became jealous of their position or lack of recognition in the church.

But more to my thinking, and in my experience, there are so many examples of those who have kept the trust. People right here in this congregation, heroes of faithfulness. I could tell you so many stories about sacrificial giving, or confidence through physical suffering, or courage throughout humiliation or bereavement, or holding on in the midst of worldly failure, doubt, and estrangement. But, to avoid embarrassment, let me tell you of Donald Tippett who was a Bishop of the United Methodist Church serving the San Francisco area. If you had seen him during his episcopacy, you would notice that one of his eyes drooped badly.

Years before, Donald Tippett was a minister in New York City. Two young thugs conducted a robbery in up-state New York, and to establish an alibi they ingeniously decided to visit a pastor. Rev. Tippett received them in good faith, but as he chatted with them, he received a phone call that he took in another room. They became suspicious, thinking he had been informed of the robbery, and they attacked him there in his office. His left eye was mangled with a set of brass knuckles.

Afterward the thieves were apprehended, and the minister pleaded in their behalf. He got their sentence reduced, visited them in prison, and planned their "after life." One of them, he helped through college and medical school. Of all things, the young assailant became an ophthalmologist.

Tippett would have said it was nothing spectacular, that he just stood by two troubled young men. But Jesus would have said, "It is people like you . . . all of you, serving in many different ways. **You are the ones who have stood by me through my trials.**"

Nothing is more important than to hear the ones you love say, "You stood by me." It is a compliment that has real force and power! So I implore you to take heart, be of good cheer; this Jesus, who gave His life for us, and yet who lives, and who loves us most of all, this Lord of Lords is saying to you, hopefully to every one of you, "**You are the ones, who stood by me through my trials.**"

In the name of Christ, *Amen.*

NOTES

1   Overstreet, Bonaro, *Stubborn Ounces.*

2   McCullough, Donald W., *Waking From the American Dream*, 1988, p. 181.

3.

Ministers of Grace

I preached often about the marvelous grace of God, and when I was asked to preach at the Contemporary Service at Dauphin Way on July 31, 2011, I returned to that gracious theme. Preaching in the Contemporary Service was a new experience and a wonderful experience, almost like being at a campsite or retreat: such a relaxed and informal atmosphere. For the first time in many years, I preached with no coat, no tie, sleeves rolled up, and so close to people that it seemed like theater in the round. I don't wonder that so many, particularly the younger generation, are attracted to this service. The occasion seemed to call for that which was basic and fundamental, so I preached on being the "Ministers of Grace":

> *Now I would remind you, brethren, in what terms I preached to you the gospel, which you received, in which you stand, by which you are saved, if you hold it fast—unless you believed in vain. For I delivered to you as of first importance what I also received, that Christ died for our sins in accordance with the scriptures, that he was buried, that he was raised on the third day in accordance with the scriptures, and that he appeared to Cephas, then to the twelve. Then he appeared to more than five hundred brethren at one time, most of whom are still alive, though some have fallen asleep. Then he appeared to James, then to all the apostles. Last of all, as to one untimely born, he appeared also to me. For I am the least of the apostles, unfit to be called an apostle, because I persecuted the church of God. But by the grace of God I am what I am, and his grace toward me was not in vain. On the contrary, I worked harder than any of them, though it was not I, but the*

grace of God which is with me. Whether then it was I or they, so
we preach and so you believed.

I CORINTHIANS 15:1–11 (RSV)

SAINT PAUL WAS ASTOUNDED at the "amazing grace" of God. In the scripture
we read today, Paul is saying, I am not worthy to be called an apostle. I
persecuted the Church of God, but even so, through His grace I have been
called to preach the unsearchable riches of Christ. Amazing! **"By the grace of
God I am what I am: and his grace which was bestowed upon me was not
in vain. . . ."** (I Corinthians 15:10) Grace was a constant theme with Paul;
he said in Ephesians (4:29), **"unto every one of us is given grace according to the measure of the gift of Christ."** When I hear that word "grace,"
I am reminded that Dr. George Buttrick said, "So much preaching today
is moralism, not the gospel. It is exhortation to better living rather than an
offering of the gracious love of God." And Dr. Albert Outler asked, "Where
should the church be concentrating its energies in the next ten to twenty-
five years?" He answered his own question. "I believe it should concentrate
on calling attention to the sovereign grace of God. I don't hear the gospel
preached in the churches I attend today."

I am not suggesting that Christians must choose between a personal
gospel and a social gospel, or that we must choose between private and
public religion, between prayer and practice. No. I believe we need a bal-
anced faith. The danger is that we concentrate on one thing and forget the
other. Kate Smith said that her mother always had trouble with her father
and the furnace; every time her mother watched one, the other would go
out! We need a full gospel—God's grace expressed in our personal life, our
church life, in our community, and in our service to others. We need a new
understanding of grace.

Grace was once a central theme in preaching and in the great hymns
of the Church:

> Come, thou fount of every blessing
> Tune my heart to sing thy grace.
> —Robert Robinson

'Twas grace that taught my heart to fear
And grace my fears relieved;
How precious did that grace appear
The hour I first believed.
      —John Newton

Thy sovereign grace to all extends,
Immense and unconfined;
From age to age it never ends,
It reaches all mankind.
      —Charles Wesley

But, what is grace? It is, of course, one of the properties of God's love. It is God's personal attitude toward us. Grace contains all we know of the good news of God. God's divine presence in our lives—*that is grace*. The forgiveness of God—*that is grace*. Divine healing—*that is grace*. Suffering transformed into hope and joy, *that is grace*. "It is God giving himself in many ways, especially in the humiliation of Jesus Christ."[1] *That is grace*. In II Corinthians (8:9), Paul returns to this central them: **"For you know the grace of our Lord Jesus Christ, that though he was rich, yet for your sake he became poor, so that by his poverty you might become rich."** That is grace!

Charisma is the Greek word we translate "grace." It means "a gift." Today we use the word "charisma" to describe an illusive quality of personal charm, a magnetism, a persuasive power, the ability to excite or to inspire one's fellow man. As we commonly use the term, it is morally neutral. Gandhi had charisma in leading the Indian people through a non-violent revolution, but Hitler, haranguing the multitudes, utilizing propaganda and persuasion to control Nazi Germany, had charisma as well.

The way we use the term, some folks have it; some folks don't. I remember one preacher described as "personality-minus." When he entered the room you felt like someone just left. He didn't have it! Strictly speaking, all of that is a misuse of the word, charisma. Charisma is a Christian word, a New Testament word, a word scarcely known in classical Greek. Paul uses the term seventeen times in Romans alone! Charisma, "a gift from God." It is the word we translate "grace."

Remember that Paul says, "**Unto everyone of us is given grace, according to the measure of the gift of Christ.**" (Ephesians 4:7) No one is left out! It is not an accidental matter. Some folks have it, some folks don't? No! The gift is measured out to everyone according to the rich diversity of Christ. No one is overlooked. We may ignore the gift, or neglect the gift, or not even realize that we have a special gift, but every one of us who has faith and trust in the Lord Christ has been given charisma, a gift of God's grace.

> And every virtue we possess,
> And every conquest won,
> And every thought of holiness
> Are his alone.[2]

These virtues are not mine but God's grace in me! That is a wonderful truth: that God has given Himself to all who believe. He is your *charisma*, your gift of grace, your salvation, your strength, your forgiveness and your joy!

In that same chapter of Ephesians, Paul says, "**Let no corrupt communication proceed out of your mouth, but only that which is good for the use of edifying (or building up) in order that it may minister grace to the hearers.**" (4:29) Christians don't say or do anything that hurts people or that tears people down; we only build people up. One young man was so exasperated with his mother because she never criticized anybody. He said, "Mother, I think you would say something good about the Devil himself." She said, "Well, he is persistent!"

Remember, grace is not given for our personal benefit alone, but in order for us to be "**the ministers of grace.**" Here we are, at a time of political division, economic uncertainty, natural disaster, and global conflict; there is personal suffering everywhere. Think what it would mean if every Christian became a minister of grace. You see, ministry is for everyone; it is not just for preaching, it is for every kind of Christian service.

Christian worship is a ministry of grace. Every time we gather together in worship, we celebrate God's gift of grace, and we must offer to others that gift. After a busy week in the secular world, it is important to be reminded of the power of God and of how completely we are dependent on His grace, to be assured that we have received it, and that we share it. Through the sermon, the music, the prayers, and the graciousness of the people, everyone who attends true worship should be able to feel the gracious acceptance of God.

In the Roman Catholic Church, the Holy Communion is called the "Eucharist." (Hear the word *charis*?) The service is thanksgiving for the gift of grace, because the Holy Communion is the greatest gift: **"This is my body given for you. . . ."** In John's gospel, Jesus said, **"He that believeth on me hath everlasting life. I am that bread of life. The bread that I will give is my flesh, which I will give for the life of the world."** (John 6:47–48, 51) It is the great gift of grace!

I shall never forget going unannounced to a Roman Catholic retreat house called Holy Trinity. It is on the eastern boundary of our state, between Eufaula and Phenix City. I was looking for a place where Methodist preachers could hold a spiritual retreat. I did not know a thing about Holy Trinity, except that it was operated by the Roman Catholics. I arrived cautiously. I saw some of the nuns and wondered if I, being both male and Methodist, would be welcome. I knocked with some fear and trembling, and asked to see the director. The director of the house was Sister Rita Holmes, who said that I was most welcome. She said they wished Holy Trinity to be a place where any Christian could come for spiritual retreat.

I was then introduced to the priest who was leading the current retreat and invited to stay for mass, which was about to begin. It was a beautiful but informal service. The music was by guitar, the liturgy was in English, and there were spontaneous prayers. Someone would say, "Pray for peace," and all would respond, "Lord, teach us to pray." Then someone would say, "Pray for the missionaries," and they would respond, "Lord teach us to pray." Then, to my surprise, someone said, "Pray for our friend, The Reverend Stephen Dill," and again they responded, "Lord, teach us to pray."

My soul! I felt included.

As we had entered the chapel, each person had placed on the paten a communion wafer that was later taken to the altar to be blessed and distributed. I did not add a wafer, because, not being Roman Catholic, I knew I was not to receive the Holy Eucharist, the gift of grace. I was sitting beside Sister Rita, and when it was her turn to go to the altar, I moved to let her by, but she did not go. She whispered to me: "Here is where we are divided; our practice has not caught up with our theology. So I have determined not to receive the elements of the Holy Eucharist until we can receive them together." Now that was a tremendous gift given to me, a stranger—to deny herself "the gift of grace," until we could, in Christian unity, partake together of the grace of God.

Driving home that night, I still felt the wonder of it. I asked myself, what was the euphoria I was feeling, what was this gift of grace? I decided that I had simply been in church; that's all. I had been with Christian people, and Christians offer to others, even strangers, the gift of God's grace. That is what people need to feel every time they worship—members, strangers, everyone—that they are welcome, that they are being cared for, and that they are offered God's gracious gift. You and I must be sure that our worship is a ministry of grace!

At home, at school, at work—in our daily lives—we must be the ministers of grace. If we were to be asked, "What is the goal of your life? What is it you want out of life?" most of us would answer, "to be fulfilled as a person," or "to realize success," or "to reach my highest potential." But, if Saint Paul had been asked that question before his conversion, he would have answered, "righteousness." It was the goal of any conscientious Jew to be justified before God as righteous, having kept the Law. But later, when Paul understood the gift of Christ, then he knew that the goal and purpose of life was to realize that we are not justified by our works, but by God's gift of grace, and that our purpose is to live in gratitude for grace, to love Him and serve Him. **"For by grace you have been saved through faith, and that not of yourselves; it is the gift of God. . . ."** (Ephesians 2:80)

Paul thought of it this way: in our own strength, we can never measure up. Try to earn our salvation, and we ask for failure. When we try to be righteous, we become self-righteous. Try to be perfect in everything, we feel like failures! If we have to earn our worth by our deeds, our deeds will always be self-serving. All efforts to justify our own existence fall short. However, when we believe that God cares for us in spite of our rebelliousness, when we trust his grace to change our motivation from duty to love, we discover what it means to be righteous—*justified*—to be right with God. Then, as ministers of God's grace, we earnestly desire to share the gift, to do all the good we can because of His great love toward us. Faith through grace is righteousness.

I frequently meet people who are trying to do enough to be "worth something" to somebody else—children trying to be smart enough or good enough, wives trying to be pretty enough, husbands trying to be rich enough! Why can't we be the ministers of grace at home, and in our daily lives? Why can't we let the ones we love know we love them, not for what they do to please us, but simply because of who they are, beloved children of God? This grace—this amazing grace—would bring real happiness to our families, our friends, and to ourselves.

Ken Olsen, a Christian psychologist, wrote a book called *The Art of Hanging Loose in an Uptight World*.[3] Olsen had always tried to be perfect. Failure for him was a tremendous loss of self-esteem. In time he came to realize this was not just a psychological problem but a religious problem. Olsen grew up in Phoenix and played high school football under the legendary Walt Ruth who was called "the Vince Lombardi of high school football." Ruth demanded one hundred percent dedication from his players; he was a tremendously successful coach and would not tolerate failure. Olson played defensive halfback. In one of the first games of his senior year, the end on the opposite team got behind him and caught a touchdown pass that won the game. Olson was humiliated!

It got worse! The next day, his picture was on the front page of the paper, arms outstretched trying to block the pass. It was devastating. Then, what he feared most happened. On Monday morning, when he arrived at school, he was told the coach was waiting to see him. When he entered the coach's office, the newspaper, opened to his picture, was on the desk.

"What do you have to say about this picture?" asked Coach Ruth. "I'm sorry," said Olsen. "I'll try harder." Ruth said, "Ken, look at the picture again, look closely this time. Look at your face. Look at your muscles. Can't you see that's your problem? You are trying too hard now! I want you to relax. I want you to believe in yourself and enjoy the game. You are going to be a great player."

Ken Olsen said it was a gift of grace. Let us be the ministers of grace, reminding our friends and family, and even strangers that, **"Unto every one of us is given grace, according to the measure of the gift of Christ."** (Eph. 4:7)

Now, it becomes *extremely* difficult. We are charged to be the ministers of grace to our *enemies*! That's tough. There was an account on ABC Television of the anniversary celebration commemorating the action of Dr. Baruch Goldstein. He was the Jewish physician who, on February 25, 1994, killed forty Muslims while they were at prayer in the Cave of the Patriarchs at Hebron. This tomb is the burial place of Abraham and Sarah, sacred to Judaism, Islam and Christianity; it was once a synagogue, then a mosque, now both at once. It is the only place in the world where Jews and Muslims pray side by side.

ABC News interviewed a young lad of about twelve years old who had been there the year before and witnessed the murder of his father. The interview was conducted from the young man's own balcony from which he could see the commemoration of that horrific event. The young man was articulate and composed. He said, "Those people are crazy, and when I am older I will do to them what they did to my father."

It is all so sad and continuous, this endless cycle of revenge. One of the radical Jewish spokesmen said something I could not forget. He said, "Revenge is the sanctification of God." It is so tragic! Let me quickly say those attitudes do not represent all the Jews nor all the Muslims by any means. There are, on both sides, people who long for peace, and who work for peace. And I must say this: revenge is not the sanctification of God. The sanctification of God, the holiness of God, is perfect love; it is grace personified in the sacrifice of Christ!

It is so difficult to be a minister of grace to the ones who have mistreated us. Our Lord said, **"You have heard it said, an eye for and eye and a tooth for a tooth. But I say to you, love your enemies, do good to those who hate you, bless those who curse you, pray for those who abuse you. . . . Be perfect** (Luke 6:27–36) or, **"Be merciful even as you Father is merciful."**

(Matthew 5:38–48) Or you could put it this way, "Let all believers be full of grace, just as your Father in heaven is full of grace." It is not easy to be a minister of grace!

No, it is not easy, but through faith and prayer it is *possible*. Many years ago a gentleman came to me with an unusual request. He explained that forty years before, he had worked for a family in our church and had stolen some money from them. He did not wish to die with that on his conscience. He said he had taken a small amount of cash from the register, intending to pay it back. But soon he took more and then more, until he *could not* pay it back. He said, "I knew I was a better man than that, and being unable to repay them, I resigned. That was forty years ago." He then asked me to set up a meeting with the family so that he could confess, ask for their forgiveness, and repay his debt with interest.

The next Sunday, we met in my office after church. It was a most impressive meeting. The first thing the family did was to embrace him without a word. He was so nervous that he could only read a prepared statement. It described what he had done, asked for their forgiveness, and expressed his desire to repay his debt. The spokesman for the family said, "We have always remembered you fondly. We thought a great deal of you then; we think even more of you now. If you took anything from us, consider it a gift. You don't owe us anything. If it would help you to repay something, that's fine; but we don't wish to know about it. You know the charities we are interested in." That was a moment of grace! The next day the gentleman brought me a generous contribution for the Methodist Children's Home.

"Ministers of grace." What a noble company they are . . . you are! A company of those who have received the forgiveness of God and the mercies of Christ, and who in turn are so transformed as to offer to others the gift of God's grace.

> Grant us such grace
> That we may speak thy word,
> And work thy will,
> And walk before thy face

Profound and calm like waters deep and still.

Dear God, Grant us such grace.[4]

In the name of Christ, *Amen.*

Notes

1   Dale Moody, *The Word of Truth*, Wm. B. Eerdmans Pub., Co. 1981, p. 106.

2   Auber, Harriet, "Our Blest Redeemer, Ere He Breathed", # 177 *The Methodist Hymnal*, The Methodist Publishing House, Nashville, Tenn., 1932.

3   Olsen, Ken, *The Art of Hanging Loose in an Uptight World*, Revell, 1984, p. 143f.

4   Christina Rossetti, *Gifts and Graces.*

4.

The King of Glory

In July of 2000, having served for ten years as Senior Minister of Dauphin Way, The Rev. Dr. Benjamin Michael Watson was elected to the episcopacy. Before he left to attend the Southeastern Jurisdictional Conference where bishops were to be elected, Dr. Watson asked me to preach while he was away. It was my task to prepare a sermon for Sunday, July 19, 2000, not knowing whether or not Dr. Watson would be chosen. Fortunately for the United Methodist Church, B. Michael Watson was elevated to the episcopacy. An episcopal election is such an auspicious occasion that I decided to preach on "The King of Glory":

> *The earth is the LORD'S, and the fullness thereof; the world, and they that dwell therein. For he hath founded it upon the seas, and established it upon the floods. Who shall ascend into the hill of the LORD? Or who shall stand in his holy place? He that hath clean hands, and a pure heart; who hath not lifted up his soul unto vanity, nor sworn deceitfully. He shall receive the blessing from the LORD, and righteousness from the God of his salvation. This is the generation of them that seek him, that seek thy face, O Jacob.*
>
> *Lift up your heads, O ye gates; and be ye lift up, ye everlasting doors; And the King of glory shall come in. Who is this King of glory? The LORD strong and mighty, the LORD mighty in battle. Lift up your heads, O ye gates; even lift them up, ye everlasting doors; And the King of glory shall come in. Who is this King of glory? The LORD of hosts, he is the King of glory.*
>
> PSALM 24 (KJV)

OUR MINDS AND HEARTS are filled with different emotions today at Dauphin Way, but congratulations and celebration lead the list. The Southeastern Jurisdiction of the United Methodist Church met last week and elected three new Bishops, Larry M. Goodpaster from Tupelo, Mississippi, who has been assigned to the Alabama/West Florida Area, James R. King, Jr. from Brentwood, Tennessee, who was the beloved pastor of my son Stuart and his family, and our own Benjamin Michael Watson.

The lives of Mike and Margaret Watson have already changed dramatically. They will be moving to south Georgia. Their lives will never be the same. It has been said that election to the episcopacy marks the last time the bishop will hear the truth or get a bad meal. From this point on, Bishop Watson will concern himself with issues that relate to the church at large and shape our denomination in the future. His decisions will affect the lives of ministers and the welfare of congregations for the whole church, but particularly in the South Georgia Conference. This is not an easy task, and we pray for Mike to have wisdom and vision, sensitivity and compassion as he leads the church in this wider connection.

We congratulate the Church on its wisdom, and we congratulate Bishop Benjamin Michael Watson! He brings to the office of bishop a rich background of opportunity and experience, he brings such natural gifts and graces that are pleasing to God and to the church, and above all he brings an energetic dedication to perform the work of Christ.

The year of General Conference with its legislative power and the election of bishops at the Jurisdictional Conference is always a pivotal, critical time for United Methodists. At Dauphin Way, we have followed the proceedings of the Jurisdictional Conference with more than usual interest since our pastor was one of the episcopal nominees. The election of bishops has always captured the attention of the church. There is personal drama involved; there are resulting changes in appointments. There are theological implications with God choosing the leadership of the church; the prosperity and the direction of the denomination are at stake.

I would argue that in a strange way, these diverse considerations all spring from the same basic premise: what we really want is an experience with God. Behind all these questions and procedures is the search for what we truly desire. We want the assurance that God is involved, we want an experience with the Almighty.

This is an exciting time. These weeks and months have witnessed many prayers for God's guidance on behalf of both Michael Watson and Dauphin Way. And, of course, the resulting Service of Consecration is surrounded by many celebrations. With that in mind, I have chosen as our lesson for today a passage taken out of the hymnal of ancient Judaism.

The 24th Psalm is a processional hymn used to recognize and celebrate God's enthronement as King of the world. Ever since that first festival when David brought the Ark of the Covenant to Jerusalem, believers have used this psalm to celebrate the approach of the Almighty. The first celebration was uninhibited; it was truly a celebration. There was shouting and blowing of trumpets, and David the king **danced before the Lord with all his might.**" (II Samuel 6:14, KJ) He "**danced without restraint before the Lord.**" (NEB)

Can you imagine that procession approaching the City of David, singing, "Lift up your heads, O ye gates, and be ye lifted up ye everlasting doors, and the King of glory shall come in!" A voice responds, "Who is this King of glory?" And the chorus answers, "The Lord strong and mighty! The Lord mighty in battle! Lift up your heads, O ye gates, lift them up ye everlasting doors, and the King of glory shall come in."

In all the processions and pageantry of the Church with their liturgy and protocol, throughout all the impressive conferences of world leaders in the midst of the crowds and grandeur, we must never consider the attending glory to be our own. If there is a transcendent glory, a true and everlasting glory, then it is God's glory and not ours. The glorious presence of God, which comes upon us either publicly or privately, causes us to fall upon our knees and cry, "Unclean! Unclean!" and to realize that all earthly glory is but a passing fancy. "Who is the King of glory? The Lord of hosts, he is the King of glory!"

On so many occasions when glorious worship was concluded at Dauphin Way, I would stand at the rear of the sanctuary and look down the aisle at the altar, the stained glass window, and the silent congregation, as the choir sang the closing doxology. I would think: How important it is for me to be away from the center, outside, in the vestibule. It cannot be my glory; it is God's glory.

Sometimes the Church is confused, thinking that power, authority, wealth, prestige, and order are the marks of divine glory. But they are not! The Lord Christ was crucified, glorified in weakness, in suffering, in self-giving. The Lord said to Saint Paul, "My power is made perfect in weakness." (II Corinthians 12:9) There is a tradition that when Saint Dominic visited Rome, the Pope showed the poor monk the magnificence of the Holy Church. The Pope said, "No longer can the church say 'Silver and gold have I none.'" Quietly Saint Dominic replied, "Neither can it say, 'Arise and walk.'"[1] The glory of the Church must be the same glory as the glory of its Lord.

Martin Luther said one time, "The great and worldly-wise people take offence at the poor and mean form of our church which is subject to many infirmities. They say the church should be altogether pure, holy, and blameless. And the church, in the eyes and sight of God, has such an esteem; but in the eyes and sight of the world, she is like unto her bridegroom, Christ Jesus, torn, spit on, derided and crucified."[2]

Notice what is already happening! The moment we read this psalm we are lifted out of the past into the present. Immediately we realize that we are addressed, not some ancient city of long ago. We ourselves are involved in the dialogue. The King of Glory approaches our domain; He seeks entrance to our lives and hearts. The Word of the Lord cries out to us: "Lift up your heads, O ye gates, lift them up ye everlasting doors, and the King of glory shall come in."

I believe there is an innate, human hunger to know God. All life long, from the time we were infants clutching at a sunbeam, until the time when we make our plans to leave this earthly life, we seek to know God. We go to church, we visit cathedrals, we join Bible classes, we read books, we attempt good works—all because we want to know God. We are not trying to acquire information but to have an experience.

In every culture this is a fact of human life. We may not even regard it as supernatural. We may prefer to call it art, music, or poetry rather than religion, but we human beings have persistently sought a dimension of existence that is beyond our normal lives. We search for God.

We understand that God could never fully impart His nature and His name. We understand that the sacred is too great a reality to be contained within a purely human definition. We understand that our knowledge of God will always be fleeting and ambiguous. But still, we seek to know God. We seek to be touched by transcendent reality, to reach the unreachable. That desire is fundamental, and life is not rehearsal. This earthly pilgrimage is our only opportunity to fling wide the gates and let the King of glory in. We search for God, it is our greatest and our grandest hope:

> O WORLD invisible, we view thee,
> O world intangible, we touch thee,
> O world unknowable, we know thee,
> Inapprehensible, we clutch thee.[3]

Sometimes the hunger for God seems to have gone away and left us, but it never really leaves. It is innate. We may try to bury the divine restlessness in the busyness of this world, or substitute personal ambition for divine obedience, but the hunger remains. We desire to know God! A person can live in the fast lane or in the measured pace of isolation, but it is still the same. People try to say that faith is the property of hard times, but that's not true. We are restless at all times without God.

It is not easy to talk about our thirst for God. No one likes to be pressed about it. One of our preachers said he was right in the middle of 31 flavors of Baskin Robbins ice cream, deciding between chocolate ripple and pistachio, when a stranger asked if he were saved. He said, "I just told him, 'Friend, I don't have time for that now!'" Yet deep within he could not forget the question; it struck a nerve. Under other circumstances, in a place less public, he would urgently speak of God.

In the hospital, a friend will say, "Goodness, Preacher, what are you doing here? Go down the hall and visit someone who needs you. This is a piece of cake. It's under control. All they're going to do is take out my liver and my lungs!" He is afraid the preacher will stand by his bed and pray. And what he really wants is for the preacher to stand by his bed and pray . . . but he is afraid he'll cry. Postpone it, disguise it, or pretend it doesn't matter; what we pray for is that the gates will open and the King of glory will come in.

Who is this King of glory? The answer to that is the good news of the gospels! Who is the King of glory? The apostles asked that same question. Then, one day, lepers drew near to Jesus, crying, "Unclean! Unclean!" One of the lepers confronted the Master asking for mercy, and Jesus touched him and healed him. The disciples saw His compassion and His mending grace. They saw His righteousness and care for the outcasts. And one day Jesus took a towel and washed their feet. It embarrassed them, and they protested to think He would take a servant's role. And then one day this same Jesus voluntarily took a cross and carried it to Calvary. They remembered His words: "Whoever has seen me has seen the Father." They met the risen Savior in the Upper Room, and knew the King of glory had come in.

That's astounding! "In Jesus Christ the reality of God entered into the reality of this world."[4]

There is a psychiatrist in New York who works with catatonic people. He breaks the precedent of doctors remaining separate and aloof from their patients. He moves into the ward. He places his bed in the midst of their beds. He lives the life they must live. He loves them. If they don't speak he doesn't speak either. It is as if he understands what they are feeling. He puts his arm around them. He hugs them. These unattractive, unlovable, difficult people are loved back into life. Many times the first phrase a patient speaks is, "thank you." That is very much like what God did in Christ Jesus. The Word of God became as we are, to enable us to let the King of glory in.

More than any other reason this is why Jesus said, "I will build my church," to open the human heart and let the King of glory in. The gates of Hell will not prevail against that. I met recently with a group of ministers who are considering the feasibility of proclaiming Mobile "hunger-free" in 2002, its tercentennial year, asking the churches to unite and work together in such a way that every person would be free from spiritual and physical hunger. That is the servant role of the church. The bishops are right when they describe themselves as the servants of the servants of God.

I urge you to pray for the church that it may be the church that Christ intended. Pray for Michael Watson and all the bishops, ministers, and leaders of the church, for they do have an awesome responsibility—in one sense they possess the keys that open the Kingdom of God.

There is a well-known prayer for the church by Walter Rauschenbusch that I have always loved. It begins, "O God, we pray for thy church, which is set today amid the perplexities of a changing order, face to face with a great new task. Oh, baptize her afresh in the life-giving spirit of Jesus!"[5] In every age the Church is "faced with a great new task. . . ." It may be a new evangelism, a new world order for health and peace, personal and family values. "Oh, baptize her afresh in the life-giving spirit of Jesus."

How earnestly we need to pray that prayer; pray that the Church will receive the "life-giving spirit of Jesus." Pray that the Church may be filled with the prophets' scorn of tyranny, and a Christ-like tenderness for the heavy-laden and the downtrodden. Pray that the Church will not seek its own life for fear of losing it. Pray that the Church will follow its Master along the pathway of the Cross. To faithfully follow the Lord Christ is the true glory of the Church, and it is helpful to remember that without any of the majesty and pageantry that we sometimes associate with "church," the King of glory powerfully entered into the life and ministry of the early Christians.

Faith history allows us to look back and see the great things that happened when the King of glory came. The Bible is the record of the mighty acts of God. With prayer and spiritual reflection we can see God working in our own experience. We turn to the Church to teach us how to fling open the heart-gates; we know the King of glory waits. It is Him that we long for. The King of glory delivers us from sin and death, He transforms evil into goodness, and He brings forth out of nothing something new, full of grace and truth. It is the glory of the Church to enable us to open the heart-gates and let the King of glory in.

Last Sunday in Montgomery, Alabama, we went to church with our daughter, Laurie, and her family. In church she was the typical mother of three small boys. She looked innocent and domestic. It was difficult for me to realize she is the Medical Director of Medical AIDS Outreach of Alabama (MAO). I wondered how she managed the stress of that depressing medical practice. That afternoon, I discovered a number of grief poems she had written which must be a means of coping.

> The grief is dense today, damp gray
> Mist chills shrouded skies.
> Grief clouds the sun, obscuring the familiar.
>
> Poor visibility—
> Fog grudgingly allows but dim light through,
> Reflecting all the rest as opaque glare that disorients.
>
> We know in time the Sun regains her strength,
> Evaporates thick grief, restoring clarity
> And the sparkle of ordinary light.
>
> But—today we are griefed-in.
> We hold each other close—we wait
> For such heavy grief to dissipate.[6]

I'm sure that's why she goes to church. You have to find a way for grief to dissipate. When you are all "griefed-in," it's important to open the heart-gates and let the King of glory in.

Oh, pray for the Church to be faithful to Christ, and open the way for us sinners to experience God. Pray that the Church, and all of us, might be "baptized afresh in the life-giving spirit of Jesus." And when He comes, celebrate; don't be afraid to celebrate unrestrained before the Lord.

We are so complicated. There are times when we act as though we are running away from God, hiding from Him. When what we really want is for God to find us.

> I fled him, down the nights and down the days;
> I fled him down the arches of the years;[7]

Dr. Fred Craddock told about playing hide-and-seek when he was small.

I guess we have all played it. The person who is "It" hides his eyes and counts to one hundred and then shouts, "Coming ready or not" and looks for the others. If he finds them and beats them back to base, they have to be "It."

Dr. Craddock said his sister cheated. She counted 1, 2, 3, 4, 5, 6, 7 . . . 98, 99, one hundred. But he didn't care. He was so small he could hide under the steps of the porch; she would never find him there. And she didn't. She would pass the steps on the way to the barn, come back by; pass it two or three times and never find him. He would laugh to himself. She will never find me . . . just never find me. Then he realized, "She will never find me!" So the next time she came by, he would stick out his toe—or more—until she would see it, and run to base. He would come out and brush himself off and then he would be "It."

Then Dr. Craddock asked this question "What was it I wanted? To hide from my sister? Yes, but what was it I *really* wanted?" What he *really* wanted then is the same thing that you and I really want now. We want to be found.

> Lift up your heads ye mighty gates.
> Behold the King of Glory waits.
> The King of Kings is drawing near,
> The savior of the world is here.[8]

In the name of Christ, *Amen.*

Notes

1   Chesterton, St. Thomas Aquinas, *The Dumb Ox*, Image Books, 1956.
2   Luther, Martin, *Table Talk of Martin Luther*, The World Publishing Co., 1952, p. 226.
3   Thompson, Francis, *The Hound of Heaven*.
4   Bonhoeffer, Dietrich, *Ethics*, Stott, p. 189.
5   Rauschenbusch, *Prayers of the Social Awakening*, Pilgrim Press, 1910.
6   Dill, M. D., Laurie E., "Griefed-In."
7   Thompson, Francis, *The Hound of Heaven*.
8   Weissel, George, *1642*.

5.

The Wings of Madness

In 2009, The Rev. Dr. Gorman Houston, beloved Senior Minister of Dauphin Way United Methodist Church in Mobile, Alabama, suddenly resigned from the church and from the ministry. His resignation was traumatic for the congregation and a significant loss to the United Methodist Church. Dr. Houston is greatly loved, and he is remarkably blessed with the "gifts and graces" necessary for pastoral ministry. On the Sunday after his resignation, in a beautiful act of graciousness and courage, Dr. Houston, as a layman, united with the congregation he had so ably served as pastor. On that occasion I preached "The Wings of Madness":

> *Now Moses was keeping the flock of his father-in-law, Jethro, the priest of Midian; and he led his flock to the west side of the wilderness, and came to Horeb, the mountain of God. And the angel of the LORD appeared to him in a flame of fire out of the midst of a bush; and he looked, and lo, the bush was burning, yet it was not consumed. And Moses said, "I will turn aside and see this great sight, why the bush is not burnt." When the LORD saw that he turned aside to see, God called to him out of the bush, "Moses, Moses!" And he said, "Here am I."*
>
> *Then he said, "Do not come near; put off your shoes from your feet, for the place on which you are standing is holy ground." And he said, "I am the God of your father, the God of Abraham, the God of Isaac, and the God of Jacob." And Moses hid his face, for he was afraid to look at God. Then the LORD said, "I have seen the affliction of my people who are in Egypt, and have heard their cry because of their taskmasters; I know their sufferings, and I*

have come down to deliver them out of the hand of the Egyptians,
and to bring them up out of that land to a good and broad
land, a land flowing with milk and honey, to the place of the
Canaanites, the Hittites, the Amorites, the Perizzites, the Hivites,
and the Jebusites. And now, behold, the cry of the people of Israel
has come to me, and I have seen the oppression with which the
Egyptians oppress them. Come, I will send you to Pharaoh that
you may bring forth my people, the sons of Israel, out of Egypt. "
But Moses said to God, "Who am I that I should go to Pharaoh,
and bring the sons of Israel out of Egypt?" He said, "But I will be
with you; and this shall be the sign for you, that I have sent you:
when you have brought forth the people out of Egypt, you shall
serve God upon this mountain. "

EXODUS 3:1–12 (RSV)

I KNOW IT IS shocking to you—it certainly is to me—to find me once again in the pulpit of Dauphin Way, twenty years after my retirement. There is something not right about it. Shakespeare would have said, "the time is out of joint."[1] It is strange and totally unexpected. All of us are having a difficult time, but with our faith in God and with God's good grace we will manage to find our way. It is important that we learn how to cope with moments of extremity—sudden and surprising developments that leave us without words, leave us wondering how and why the meaning of life has abruptly disappeared. Too often we are left with the unanswerable question: how do we prepare for the unexpected?

I was at Huntingdon College on the morning of September 11, 2001, when we learned of the suicide attacks by al-Qaeda on the World Trade Center. Both towers collapsed in two hours; 2,973 victims died, Americans to be sure, but also nationals from ninety countries. I was proud of the quick response of the college: almost immediately a giant TV screen without sound was set up in the chapel where the students gathered. The chaplain spoke about grief; professors who had lived in targeted areas spoke on coping with extremism; other professors related the history of fanaticism. Counselors were available, and students with family in New

York were assisted in contacting them. Still, with all that, we were numbed and shocked, trying to make sense of it all. It reminded me of a line by the French poet, Charles Baudelaire: "Today I felt pass over me a breath of wind from the wings of madness."[2]

I had felt that way before: at the assassination of President Kennedy, during Hurricane Katrina, the tsunami in Samoa, the earthquake in Haiti and now Chile, the death of a friend—all devastating events, unforeseen and bewildering. I feel it again today, "Today I felt pass over me a breath of wind from the wings of madness."

Sometimes that madness takes the form of an ungrounded fear that leaves us spent after a sleepless night, dreading that which will never happen. Or it is the time you witnessed a conversation that became so irrational, so totally out of balance, filled with such hatred and ugliness, that you felt that wind from the wings of madness.

In these weeks of worship during Lent, the church has focused on the study of the Exodus. We are reviewing the mighty acts of God that led the Israelites from slavery to freedom, and how God chose Moses to make that happen. The Bible says, **"And there has not arisen a prophet since in Israel, like Moses, whom the Lord knew face to face . . ."** (Deut. 34:10)

Moses is the most commanding figure of the Old Testament. He is the deliverer and the lawgiver for his people. "Condensed into this one man are the figures of prophet, priest, judge, lawgiver, intercessor, victor, exile, fugitive, shepherd, guide, healer, miracle-worker, man of God, and rebel. Moses does not merely assist at the birth of Israel, in him Israel is born,"[3] and, in addition to all that, Moses represents the whole *future* of Israel.

Life was not smooth and easy for Moses. He found himself rejected, a fugitive and forced to flee from his Egyptian life of privilege to a desert wilderness on the back side of Mount Sinai. Then, of all things, Moses was drawn to a phenomenon he could not explain: a bush that was burning and burning but was not consumed!

When Moses turned aside for a closer look, God called his name. How awesome is that! God said, "Moses, this dismal, barren place where you are standing right now, is Holy Ground."

I tell you, *we* need to hear that. God doesn't need a special time or a special place to reach into the human heart. Where you are right now is Holy Ground.

While Moses was captivated by the burning bush, God revealed His own identity: **"I am the God of your father, the God of Abraham, the God of Isaac, the God of Jacob." And God said, "I have observed the misery of my people . . . I have heard their cry . . . I know their suffering."** Isn't that amazing! "How light and portable my pain seems now, when that which makes me bend, makes the King bow."[4] And God added, "I will deliver my people from bondage, Moses, and I will use you to do it."

It is no wonder Moses hid his face and began to make excuses. This was a totally awesome and unexpected experience. He was in no way prepared to confront the Pharaoh, much less to come face to face with God. I have always thought it was to Moses' credit that he did not panic! He saw the burning bush and heard the voice of God, but he did not run away and cry, "It's a mad, mad world." Curious, if nothing else, he followed the incredible signpost of the Almighty.

Now here we are at worship, worship so familiar and yet so strange and unusual, it is as if we were in the midst of a barren wilderness. Nevertheless, we are certain that God is working here and now. Startling as it may be to us, we are ready to listen for God to call our name, to tell us who He is and what He wants us to do. To some of us the wilderness is new. Some of us may have been in the wilderness a long time; we may have settled for the mediocrity of life and the absence of God until this day when something stirred within us, and our hearts burned for God like the burning bush.

We have learned from Moses that a commission from God comes with the promise of His presence. When Moses pressed God to tell him His name in order to understand His nature and His power, the Almighty answered, **"Say to the people of Israel, I AM has sent me to you."** Martin Buber, the great Jewish scholar, says the verb is dynamic and should be translated "I will be present when I will be present,"[5]

So, here we are at worship, in search of a certain strength of character, a nobility of spirit, a calmness and trust that is only practiced by those persons who have the courage to stand in the presence of the Almighty, those who know that the great I AM is always present.

Saint Augustine, Bishop of Hippo, wrote *The City of God* in order to restore the confidence of his fellow Christians after the sack of Visigoths in AD 410! Augustine wrote, "The tide of trouble tests, purifies, and improves the good, whereas it beats, crushes, and washes away the wicked."[6] He said, Christians know that from the one, true, and infinitely good God they have a nature by which they are made in His image, a faith by which they know God and themselves, and a grace by which they reach a blessed union with a loving Father.

It is no wonder the Bible admonishes us to fix our attention upon God—to look beyond ourselves and this earthly city and look toward Him. Just like the old hymn says:

> Turn your eyes upon Jesus,
> Look full in His wonderful face,
> And the things of earth will grow strangely dim,
> In the light of His glory and grace.[7]

There is such power in the hymnal, and the Book of Psalms is the hymnbook of ancient Israel. The Book of Psalms has been called the "mirror of the soul" because it clearly reflects our human condition, our sinfulness and depression, our sense of wonder and of praise, and it shines forth God's grandeur and His mercy. At the beginning of worship we read together the 19th Psalm, praising God for His glorious creation of the natural world, and even more for His ordering of the moral law: "**The heavens declare the glory of God and the firmament showeth his handiwork . . . The law of the Lord is perfect, reviving the soul.**" Psalm 19 ends with this heartfelt benediction: "**Let the words of my mouth and the meditation of my heart, be acceptable in thy sight, O Lord, my strength and my redeemer.**"

There is only one secret to spiritual strength, only one claim to peace beyond calamity, and that is to keep our thoughts inwardly, and our actions outwardly, in harmony with the will of God. That's what Moses learned at the burning bush, and what we must learn today as our hearts burn in holy worship. In that mysterious encounter is found the mastery of life. The future is uncertain and unknown, but there is so much mysterious power in the worship of the Almighty that we must learn to put our trust in Him.

You may know there is some uncertainty in retirement. When I retired twenty years ago, after standing before you for eighteen years, I would sit in the congregation uninvolved and unattached, and yet what great peace I felt, surrounded by people who cared for me because they cared for God. (Gorman, I hope you can feel that love today.)

It is also true that the unexpected happens when we worship God. It happens warmly and silently as if something were burning in our hearts. I remember once at a conference at Blue Lake, I was touched by the sermon that we should be like Moses, available to God. "I felt my heart was strangely warmed." After worship, I walked up to a group, and they were not rude, but they did not include me. So I just sat on a ping-pong table and waited for a while, being available to God. Almost as if on cue, one of the ministers came to me and said "I've been waiting to see you. I want you to come and preach for me. I need the time to talk to you." So I went to preach, but I went more out of concern for the preacher than for the people. We look toward God to discover the mastery and the mystery of life.

Look toward God in order to discover the meaning of life. Willie Loman in *Death of a Salesman* kept saying: "I have the right to know who I am," and we all do. His mistake was that he kept looking inward, always at himself, never looking away from himself toward God. So he found nothing worth living for. The Christian faith assures us that life has real meaning, but it is God's meaning not our meaning.

Take the question of suffering: Why did this happen to me? This past week, in a staff meeting devotional, Jim Bell quoted Leslie Weatherhead. Weatherhead said, "God allows suffering because he wants the human family to learn, to substitute knowledge for its ignorance, wisdom for its folly, and holiness for its sin: and these three exchanges cannot be imposed on human nature. They have to be achieved by the hard way of learning."[8] But God would not *allow* a situation to befall us that would defeat His purpose ultimately. So the very fact that He allows it to happen has a hidden treasure. If he allows it, He means to use it for our good. That's why we look toward God, even in suffering, to find life's hidden treasure, to find life's meaning.

When I am with God, all life has meaning.
Big things become small, and small things become great.
The near becomes far and the future is near.
The lowly and despised is shot through with glory.[9]

Look toward God in order to discover your neighbor. Do you ever get so preoccupied with your own concerns that you fail to see your neighbor's pain? I remember Dr. George Buttrick telling me about a woman in his congregation who was so miserable, so filled with pain, and constantly aware of her loneliness and neglect. She came to see the preacher frequently and was not amused by his insistence that she make a hospital call on behalf of the church. But it changed her life. She visited constantly; she became known everywhere in New York as the angel of the hospitals.

Ash Wednesday at Dauphin Way was such a meaningful service. It was the first service after learning of our pastor's resignation, but there was no mention of that. However, I looked across the congregation and saw people quietly crying. I thought of how much pain there is here and across the world. We who are in the presence of God must be sensitive to one another, take time to listen and to pray for others.

Fosdick was quite right, that an untroubled life is an uneducated life. Those who are able to deal with tragedy and with reality are not the ones who have lived a softly cushioned life, but the ones who have treated affliction as an opportunity. People all around us are hurting; it is that kind of world. We who suffer are called to be the servants of the suffering, "the wounded healers."

One time, years ago, a member of our church threatened to leave the fellowship because I had passed him in the hall and failed to speak. I'm sure I had no excuse; I was just preoccupied. I passed him, but I didn't see him. It was embarrassing. I went to his home and apologized. We became good friends; he told me his story, and I told him mine. I can't tell you how healing that was or how important it is for you to see one another with sensitive love.

But we will never be sensitive to our neighbor's need until we are able to see him as one created in God's own image, until we are able to see our neighbor as Christ saw him from the Cross.

We must look toward God if we are ever to find an inner peace. There is a beautiful story about John Wesley. A lady asked him how he would spend his time if he knew he would die at midnight the next evening. He said, "Madam, I would spend it just as I intend to now. I would preach at Gloucester tonight and tomorrow morning, at Tewkesbury in the afternoon, go to my friend Martin's house for entertainment, converse and pray with the family as usual, retire to my room at ten o'clock, commend myself to my heavenly father, lie down to rest, and wake up in glory."[10]

When he did die, at eighty-eight, he tried to sing Isaac Watts' hymn, "I'll Praise My Maker While I've Breath," but he was too weak. His last words were, "The best of all is, God is with us."

There is no greater gift that a parent might give a child than the habit of regular communion with a loving God. It is all right to admit to a child that we have clay feet so long as the child looks to God for his holiness and strength. So we must all learn to look beyond ourselves and find in God the strength and calmness to withstand the wings of madness. And knowing God, we will then **"mount up with wings as eagles, run and not be weary, walk and not faint."** (Isaiah 40:41)

In the name of Christ, *Amen.*

NOTES

1   Shakespeare, William, *Hamlet, Prince of Denmark*, Act 1, Scene 5.

2   Baudelaire, Charles, *Intimate Journals*, tr. Christopher Isherwood, Dover Books on Literature and Drama, p. 126.

3   *The Interpreter's Dictionary of the Bible*, Abingdon Press, 1962, p. 441

4   Shakespeare, William, *King Lear*, Act 3, Scene 6.

5   Buber, Martin, *Moses*, Harper & Brothers, 1958, p. 52.

6   Augustine, *The City of God.*

7   Lemmel, Helen, *Turn Your Eyes Upon Jesus.*

8   Weatherhead, Leslie, *Salute to a Sufferer*, Abingdon Press, 1962, p. 17.

9   Rauschenbusch, Walter, *The Little Gate to God.*

10   Bosley, Harold A., *Sermons on the Psalms*, p. 57.

6.

The Rest of the Story

Each system for assigning pastors to a local church has its advantages and disadvantages. I have never decided which is the best. The only system I have known intimately, personally, is the Methodist system of pastoral appointments made by the bishop in consultation with the minister and the congregation. In 2010, Dauphin Way, having had a strong history of pastoral leadership, suddenly lost its beloved senior minister, Dr. Gorman Houston, and was soon to receive the unusual appointment of Co-Senior Pastors, Dr. Jeff L. Wilson and Rev. Robin C. Wilson, a husband-and-wife team whom the congregation did not know. As Interim Senior Minister, I wanted to reassure the congregation and guide them positively through that transition, so I preached "The Rest of the Story":

> *Soon afterwards he went to a town called Nain, and his disciples
> and a large crowd went with him. ¹²As he approached the gate
> of the town, a man who had died was being carried out. He was
> his mother's only son, and she was a widow; and with her was
> a large crowd from the town. ¹³When the Lord saw her, he had
> compassion for her and said to her, "Do not weep." ¹⁴Then he
> came forward and touched the bier, and the bearers stood still.
> And he said, "Young man, I say to you, rise!" ¹⁵The dead man
> sat up and began to speak, and Jesus gave him to his mother.
> ¹⁶Fear seized all of them; and they glorified God, saying, "A great
> prophet has risen among us!" and "God has looked favorably on
> his people!" ¹⁷This word about him spread throughout Judea and
> all the surrounding country.*
>
> LUKE 7:11–17 (RSV)

46

WHEN I READ TODAY'S scripture, I found myself wishing I knew the rest of the story, and then I thought that sounded like Paul Harvey. Is anyone else old enough to remember Paul Harvey . . . "And now for the rest of the story . . ."?

A month or so before the oil spill, my eye fell on an advertisement in the newspaper. It read:

> Female crew member wanted to live aboard and work
> on a 45-ft. sailboat with world travel in mind.
> Experience helpful though not necessary.

Wouldn't you like to know the rest of that story? Well, maybe not!

One time, years ago, I was at the Annual Conference, and a lady whom I did not recognize spoke to me. She said, "I'm Ann," and I began to wrack my brain, assuming she was a member from some church where I had previously been the pastor. And then it dawned on me: she was the girl I had dated at Conference Youth Assembly when we were teenagers! (She was lovely, but what surprised me was that she was gray-headed!)

She told me a little bit of the rest of her story: she finished college, married, had two children, and was a retired schoolteacher. She had never left the small town in Florida where she was reared. I introduced her to Ruth; I think they both enjoyed that. It was fun to see her again after all those years.

Now for the rest of the story! Believe it or not, I came back from Annual Conference and went to a reception in Fairhope, across Mobile Bay. A doctor came up and said to me, "Do you remember me? You and I went to Youth Assembly together, years ago at Huntingdon College. As a matter of fact, we were competing for the same girl, but I've forgotten her name." Rather self assured, I said, "Of course I remember. Her name's Ann. I saw her last week!"

It is fascinating that so many of the greatest stories of all, the stories in the Bible, are so often incomplete. Like the story of blind Bartimaeus, sitting there begging on the road to Jericho. Bartimaeus must have been an institution. Everybody knew him. He had been there for years. He was accepted by the community, but he himself never accepted his blindness.

And when he heard that Jesus of Nazareth was passing by, he began to call out, "Jesus, thou Son of David, have mercy on me!"

Many rebuked him, told him to be silent. But he cried out all the more, "Son of David, have mercy on me." He shouted out until Jesus stopped and called to him. Bartimaeus threw off his robe and ran to Jesus, **"and Jesus said, "What would ye have me to do?" And he answered, "Sir that I would receive my sight." And Jesus said, "Go your way, for your faith has made you whole."** (Mark 10:51)

It is a marvelous account, but I always wanted to know the rest of the story. All that the Bible says is **"And immediately, he recovered his sight and followed him on the way."** (Mark 10:52) Really, wouldn't you like to know how he used his sight. What he said, what he saw, where he followed Jesus, how long he followed Jesus, Was he as determined to heal others as he had been to find healing for himself?

Or take for instance that man with the withered hand who was in the synagogue on the Sabbath. The legalists were all around, and they were the focus of the story. They wanted to see whether Jesus would break the law and heal someone on the Sabbath. Their concern for the law destroyed their compassion, and it angered Jesus. So He said to the man, "Stretch out your hand," and at that moment his hand was restored. (Mark 3:1–6)

But we don't know the rest of the story. Nothing is said about how he used his hand. Whether he used it to build up or to tear down. Whether he used it to lift the burdens of the oppressed or to wield a heavy hand against anyone who opposed him. The Bible just does not tell us the rest of the story.

Look at the lesson for today. It is one of the most beautiful stories in all of scripture: Jesus raising the widow's son. Jesus was entering the city of Nain, followed by His disciples and a great crowd. And just as the Lord of life was entering the city gates, a young man who had died was being carried out, followed by his mother, the professional mourners, and a crowd of friends. These two great processions met each other, one bearing life and the other death.

In the midst of all that confusion, the noise and the jostling crowds are forgotten and the story focuses on Jesus and the mourning mother. The scripture says that the young man was the only son of his mother, and she was a widow. That means that he was her only support, he was all she had left to shield her from a life of poverty and destitution. The occasion marked the pathos of this present world. In Shelley's "Lament for Keats" he said:

> as long as skies are blue
> and fields are green,
> evening must usher night, and
> night urge the morrow;
> month follow month with woe,
> and year wake year to sorrow.

But the Lord Christ was flooded with compassion, and He stopped the movement of both processions, His own and the other. He touched the bier, and the bearers stopped. He went to the mother and said, "Don't weep." And then the Master of Life spoke to the widow's son, "I say to you, arise!" Immediately the young man sat up and began to speak. What a magnificent moment! And then the scripture simply says, "He gave him back to his mother."

This tender and beautiful story has so much to say about the compassion of Jesus, the power of Christ, the worth of this present life, and the hope we have for the life to come. You can almost hear the Master say, "**Because I live, you shall live also.**"

The concept of a compassionate God was not the accepted belief in antiquity. The noblest faith of that time was Stoicism, and Stoics believed that if anyone could stir your emotions, if anyone could somehow make you feel, then they could control you, and they were greater than you. Therefore, since no one was greater than God, God had no feelings whatsoever. For the Stoic, the reality of God was *apathy*. No feeling!

The raising of the widow's son is just the opposite; it is a marvelous revelation, assuring us of the tenderness of God, as we see the Son of God moved with compassion. It speaks of human pathos and the mercy of God, but it never tells us the rest of the story. Wouldn't you like to know how this young man lived out his second chance? Was he grateful or was he forgetful? Did he take care of his mother or did he take care of himself? Was he changed? Was he compassionate? Did he follow the Master? We just don't know. The Bible doesn't tell us anything about that.

These mighty acts of God recorded in the scripture leave us speechless and frustrated, because we do not know the rest of the story. However, we must realize that these accounts are not valuable because they are biography, but because they are the good news of God. They are not written for our education but for our salvation. The Biblical stories reveal the power and the purpose and the presence of God for you and me, here and now. The importance of what happened to an individual in the biblical time is diminished, because a grace is being offered for all time. God's new creation is breaking into the old order, time is irrelevant, rebirth is happening continuously. The question is not what happened to the widow's son, but what is happening to you and me. We open the Bible in order to open the book of our lives. We do not read the scripture so much as the scripture reads us, and we become the rest of the story.

So the real question is not what happened to the widow's son, but what about you? How were you reborn, how are you living out your new life in Christ? What prayers have you had answered? What blessings have you received? What are your miracles? You see, the Bible demands that we answer two questions about ourselves: How did we come to faith in God? And how will we live out our Christian experience? What is the rest of the story?

It's marvelous the way God works in our lives. He says to one, "What would have me do?" To another, He says, "Do not weep," and to another, "Arise and live." Sometimes we come to faith through joy and sometimes through great difficulty just as did Saint Paul with his infirmity. God said to Paul, "No healing for you. My grace is all you need." Faith may come to us through agonizing moments of suffering and pain.

I remember one Christmas when I was young, just at that age where my imagination was unbridled and unrealistic, and I needed to come to terms with the reality of life. In those days there was a small box on the front page of the newspaper that each day read:

19 SHOPPING
DAYS 'TIL
CHRISTMAS!

And then,

18 SHOPPING
DAYS 'TIL
CHRISTMAS!

And I knew that my parents saw that box, and they were busy shopping for me. I waited with great anticipation, listing to myself all the wonderful things that I might receive.

That Christmas was the first time I remember walking out alone to make certain that I had my emotions under control. There wasn't very much for Christmas that year; a hunting knife, I remember, under the tree. That was all.

It was a faith experience for me. I didn't know it then; I know it now. What was uppermost in my mind was to not let my parents see my disappointment, because I knew how much they loved me. I came to realize in that silent walk, that they were hurting too, and I knew there was nothing more important than the bond of love between us. And because of that loving bond, the future would be all right.

That experience helped me understand the pain and the suffering God must feel when He is limited from giving His children everything they desire and yet still hopes to maintain their love and trust.

Nels Ferré, a Christian theologian and philosopher, tried to build a system of thought based on Christianity's central reality, that God is love. He said, "I have been converted three times: the first time to conventional Christianity; the second time, to honesty; the third, to the love of God and man. The third was the real conversion; the other two were preliminary."

You must not be satisfied unless your religious experience is ever deepening. If you are simply a convert to conventional Christianity, you will someday know how inadequate that is. It will not sustain you when "month follow month with woe, and year wake year with sorrow."[1] It just won't do.

And what of honesty? It is a conversion experience when we are able to sit down and look at ourselves honestly. C. S. Lewis describes his own conversion experience saying, "For the first time, I examined myself, and what I found there appalled me: a zoo of lusts; a bedlam of ambitions; a nursery of fears; a harem of fondled hatreds. My name was Legion."[2] And he was just being honest. The real conversion is letting go of self and discovering the great joy of loving God and serving God's children with that divine love.

When the compassion of Jesus and the love of God gave the young man of Nain his life again, and he was given back to his mother, the multitude began to glorify God saying, **"God has visited his people."** But did you notice that the young man was raised to life without any prior requirements? It had nothing to do with his faith, nor as far as we know, with the faith of his mother. None in the crowd asked Jesus to heal him, so healing was not the result of their faith. It had everything to do with the compassion and the love of God. The marvelous, limitless, boundless love of God!

> God does not point his arrows to the mark
> But shoots without direction, in the dark.
> God is not over-careful of his treasure;
> He does not stop to count nor stoop to measure.
> Pity and love unmasked are freely given;
> Nothing is sold or rented out in Heaven.
>
> God sets the wheel of loveliness in gear,
> Heedless of eyes to see or ears to hear;
> Heedless of human skill, truth to uncover . . .
> O, let us love, like God, with Love left over![3]

The limitless love of God promises a future that will be revealed *to us* and *in us*. God's future is larger than any of us individually; it has to do with God's own Kingdom; it has to do with the Church. The Church Universal is a prototype of the Kingdom of God, and the Church will exist 'til the end of time, for the good news to be proclaimed and the means of grace administered.

There is a verse we need to hear in the seasons of distress. In Romans 8:18, Paul says, **"I consider that the sufferings of this present time are not worth comparing with the glory that is to be revealed to us."** J. B. Phillips translates that verse in Romans as **"In my opinion, whatever we may have to go through now is less than nothing compared with the magnificent future God has in store for us."** (Romans 8:18)

The truth is that none of us on this earth will ever know the final accounting of God's will and pleasure. How God will justify it all is just too vast for our small minds to grasp. John Ruskin understood; he said, "Our best finishing is but coarse and blundering work after all. We may smooth, and soften, and sharpen till we are sick at heart; but take a good magnifying glass to our miracle of skill, and the invisible edge is a jagged saw, and the silky thread a rugged cable, and the soft surface a granite desert. God alone can finish; and the more intelligent the human mind becomes the more infiniteness of interval is felt between human and divine work in this respect."[4] On earth, we will never know the rest of the story, but we can be assured of a "magnificent future." We Christians can be confident, patient, long-suffering, and filled with joy!

So let me say a word about our church, about Dauphin Way. Gorman and Jeanne Houston will be moving to Tuscaloosa the first week in July. Their daughter, Lisa, lives in Tuscaloosa, and this fall, their son, young Gorman, will be an entering freshman at the University of Alabama. Gorman has accepted a teaching position in the College of Commerce and Business Administration. We will carry them in our hearts, and we will be constant in prayer for their welfare, their happiness and their continued success in the service of God.

Next Sunday we will celebrate Independence Day, and the following Sunday, July 11th, we will welcome Dr. Jeff L. Wilson and Rev. Robin C. Wilson as Co-Pastors of Dauphin Way. We will welcome their three children, Rebecca, Eleanor, and Nolen into a loving congregational family that will nurture them and watch over them. Jeff and Robin are remarkable young people, naturally talented, competently trained, and deeply committed to the life and ministry of Jesus Christ. We will tell you about them in much more detail later. But for now, let me say that in God's good pleasure, the rest of the Dauphin Way story will be a cherished one. I expect a long-term pastorate, young couples uniting with the church, children and youth growing in God's grace, and all of us maturing in our spiritual life and in our Christian service. Our new pastors, in the Dauphin Way tradition, will not only be our spiritual guides and mentors but our friends as well. We will welcome them and love them.

No one knows the future; we don't even know the results of our own faith or the final contribution of our lives. Christians walk in faithfulness and trust, leaving the results to God. All we know for certain is that God loves us and God will use our efforts to carry out His purposes. However, we can be assured of this: that God will guide us into a magnificent future . . . and that, my dear friends, is the rest of the story.

In the name of Christ, *Amen.*

NOTES

1   Shelley, Percy B, from "Adonais."

2   Lewis, C. S., *Surprised by Joy*, Harcourt Brace & Co., 1955, p. 226.

3   "Blessed To Give," poet unknown.

4   Ruskin, John, *Modern Painters*, Part IV, G. Allen, 1902, p. 115.

7.

Steady Hands in a Shaken World

We ministers speak out of our own experience, wrestle with our own doubts, search for reassurance concerning our own fears and seek strength for our own weakness. In doing so we become "wounded healers," to use Jung's term, one beggar telling another where to find bread. In that sense, most preaching is autobiographical; my preaching certainly was. Not that I constantly described the events of my life, I seldom did, but the sermon always begins with the minister speaking to himself. There is also a constant tension in the Christian faith that the minister feels more acutely than anyone; it is the struggle of how to live in an earthly and material world and at the same time be faithful to Christ. Throughout almost sixty years of ministry, years of personal and public crises, I needed God's assurance for "Steady Hands in a Shaken World":

> When you see Jerusalem surrounded by armies, then know that
> its desolation has come near. Then those in Judea must flee to the
> mountains, and those inside the city must leave it, and those out
> in the country must not enter it; for these are days of vengeance,
> as a fulfillment of all that is written. Woe to those who are
> pregnant and to those who are nursing infants in those days! For
> there will be great distress on the earth and wrath against this
> people; they will fall by the edge of the sword and be taken away
> as captives among all nations; and Jerusalem will be trampled
> on by the Gentiles, until the times of the Gentiles are fulfilled.
> There will be signs in the sun, the moon, and the stars, and on
> the earth distress among nations confused by the roaring of the
> sea and the waves. People will faint from fear and foreboding of
> what is coming upon the world, for the powers of the heavens will

be shaken. Then they will see "the Son of Man coming in a cloud"
with power and great glory. Now when these things begin to take
place, stand up and raise your heads, because your redemption is
drawing near.

Luke 21:20–28 (ESV)

ALL MY LIFE I have lived in a troubled world. I have a copy of the *New York Times* published the day I was born: May 27, 1928. It seemed to predict a quiet and peaceful era. That day, the U. S. Senate killed a bill to construct fifteen light cruisers and an aircraft carrier. That day, the foreign minister of Japan reported that his government would be "happy to collaborate with cordial good will" in a multilateral treaty to abolish war as an instrument of national policy. But regardless of these indices, peace was not to be the hallmark of the twentieth century.

The attack on Pearl Harbor occurred when I was thirteen. We entered the "Atomic Age" when I was eighteen, the Korean War when I was twenty-two. The Supreme Court decision regarding segregation came just as I finished seminary, and we entered into the Civil Rights Era. Three years later, the Vietnam War began and lasted for sixteen years. In my early ministry, Kennedy was assassinated; I was thirty-five then, and five years later it was Martin Luther King, Jr. From the close of WWII to the collapse of the Soviet Union, the Cold War lasted forty-five years. The scientific triumph of those years was to give man the power to annihilate himself and his world.

Then came the shock of September 11th, Iraq and Afghanistan, the shift of wealth from west to east, a financial collapse, genocide abroad, upheaval in the Arab world, the decline of the housing market, an oil spill in the Gulf, the rise of unemployment and the increase of national debt, both at home and around the globe. I could say with Walt Whitman that these have been "quicksand years that whirl me I know not whither." [1]

You can understand why there has always been a "withdrawal" tendency in Christianity, not unlike the isolationist movement in national politics. It is a desire to seek innocence, purity, and peace by moving away from "The Secular City." This tendency is best exemplified by the hermit monks in the Middle Ages. Simeon Stylites (d. 459) was a "pillar saint." He lived on top of a raised pillar east of Antioch, away from the world, for thirty-six years. However, I never found that hermit tendency in Christ our Lord. He was constantly withdrawing to a desert place to pray or be alone but only in order to return to the world. He was not *of* the world, but He was *in* the world.

There are notable Christians in our own experience, numbers of them like Bonhoeffer, and Kawaga, Martin Neimuller, Martin Luther King, Jr., Mother Theresa, Desmond Tutu, and Terry Waite, who would testify that a Christian cannot, should not, escape one's "Christian responsibility" during the crises and conflicts of the world.

It's important to remember that Jesus also lived in troubled times. His world was shaken too. He predicted the destruction of the Temple, the sack of Jerusalem, and the end of the age. He said, "**There will be signs in sun and moon and stars. On earth nations will stand helpless, not knowing which way to turn from the roar and the surge of the sea. Men will faint in terror at the thought of all that is coming upon the world; for the celestial powers will be shaken.**" (Luke 21:25–26) And indeed Jerusalem, the center of the world for the Hebrew faithful, was destroyed in AD 70, not more than thirty-five years after Jesus had spoken. Yet, to his own . . . listen to what Jesus says to his own: "**Now when these things begin to take place, stand up straight, lift up your heads, for your salvation is at hand.**" (Luke 21:28)

That's marvelous! What do you do when your world is shaken, and you cannot hold on to your faith any longer? You hold on anyway and your faith grows deeper, your hope grows taller, and your love grows wider, and God appears nearer and more personal than you have ever known before! That's what you do when your world is shaken—you "**stand up straight, lift up your heads, for your salvation is at hand.**" That encouraging promise, true at the end of the age when the mountains are cast to the sea, is equally true today when *our* world is shaken. The Lord's Anointed One, our Savior and our God, is nearest to us when we need Him most.

Historically, there have been three great affirmations which in times of turmoil have served to steady the people of God and remind them of those things which cannot be shaken.

The first is that God is *dependable*. That was one of the great discoveries of the early Hebrews. At a time when pagan gods were noted for their capriciousness, Jehovah revealed His constant love. "**The mercy of the Lord is from everlasting to everlasting. . . .**" (Ps. 103) "**his faithfulness is unto all generations.**" (Ps. 119) Jehovah can be trusted! He will maintain the integrity of the moral law, and He will respond to those who call upon His name. Our God will keep His promises. The Christ-event—the life, death and resurrection of Jesus—is the convincing proof of God's love: "**while we were yet sinners Christ died for us.**" (Romans 5:8)

Some years ago a dear friend of mine, a committed Christian, lost his grandson. I knew how much he suffered. It hurt him terribly, his own loss, and his inability to shield his children from sorrow. He could never understand *why*, though he still trusted God's great love. I asked him about the memorial service. All he said was, "We sang 'This Is My Father's World.'"

I thought of the words: "and though the wrong seems oft so strong, God is the ruler yet." *Why* is beyond our knowledge, but God's love is everlasting! When all other foundations are shaken, the Lord God will remain steadfast and sure.

Here is another affirmation to cling to in a shaken world. *The Church is indestructible!* "**Upon this rock I will build my church and the gates of hell shall not prevail against it.**" (Matthew 16:18) That's hard for us to believe, because we equate "church" with buildings and organization. Buildings and organization don't constitute the Church, not God's Church! The Church is the people of God, the community of the faithful. Buildings fail, structures change, congregations scatter; leaders leave. And still for all of that, the Church remains. In some form, Word and Sacrament, the good news and the means of grace, will last as long as the world lasts. There will always be a way for God's story to be told, and there will always be a way to receive the benefits of God's love.

The true Church will remain. Notice the unexpected places where the Church is finding new life, exactly where the Christian faith was thought to be done with: The Roman Catholic Church in Poland, the Orthodox and the Free Church in Russia, the Methodist Church in Estonia. Africa and Latin America are living through Pentecost. Who would have expected the Pope to be welcome in Cuba? Even in China, persecution is evidence of the vitality of the Church.

It is the same with individuals. There are those, perhaps we ourselves, who have felt distanced from God, hearts hardened, minds frozen, 'til something stirs within us and God's love is let loose again. In the wasteland of our souls we have said:

> I feel the stirrings of a gift divine:
> . . . unearthly fire,
> Lit by no skill of mine.[2]

The message of God and the means of grace will not be lost. You can hold on to that in a shaken world.

One other thing, you can depend on this: *Christian virtues are permanent.* Saint Paul says that when all else passes away, faith, hope, and love remain. These Christian virtues, these characteristics of Christ, are the dimensions of the abundant life. The good life is lived in faith, trusting God. The good life is lived in hope, looking forward to the future. The good life is lived in love, lasting forever. "God is love," and love is fundamental to every positive relationship. These Christian virtues are virtues that never end!

So I am saying these things are true and worthy of acceptance: God is dependable. His Church is forever. His love is everlasting. Because of these amazing affirmations, the Christian can take courage, and be spiritually alert, and look for God's purpose and redemption when the world is shaking. When the times are uneasy and unsettled, Christian people bring order out of chaos and goodness out of evil. They hear their Lord saying, "**stand up straight, lift up your heads, for your salvation is at hand.**"

Sir Robert Shirley lived in the troubled days of Oliver Cromwell. He was unheralded and unknown except in the little English village of Stanton-Harold. In the chapel at Stanton-Harold, one can read this inscription:

> In the year 1653 when all things sacred were,
> throughout the nation,
> either demolished or profaned,
> Sir Robert Shirley founded this church
> whose singular praise it is

to have done the best things in the worst times.

I met a Christian artist once whose only subject was the Crucifixion. He had painted a thousand different views of Christ on the cross. That was all he painted. He said he did so, because the Crucifixion was the vertical and horizontal focal point of our interaction with God. He explained that the Crucifixion reveals God's love and mercy, His patience and forgiveness, and it also displays our sinfulness and guilt. Then the artist said, "The purpose of art is to destroy the observer." If we are shaken, broken, and destroyed, God can put us back together the way He wants us.

When I was young, I remember a disagreement between my mother and my sister. It had been rather direct. They had gone off into different rooms without resolving anything. Though I was too small to understand what was happening, I knew some reconciliation was needed. Sister was sulking. She said she supposed she would have to leave home and live somewhere else. I thought Mother ought to know how serious things were, so I explained it to her. I told her what Sister had said. That just destroyed Mother, and she began to cry. Sister began to cry. I have this strange memory of being out of synch. Everyone crying and embracing and saying they were sorry, and that they loved each other—while I was dancing around laughing and applauding! I really didn't know what had happened, but I did understand that relationships had been all broken up, and now things were being put back right again.

In 1948, just after the close of World War II, Paul Tillich, the German philosopher and theologian, preached a sermon called "The Shaking of the Foundations." He had been a chaplain in the German Army in WWI, and, because of his views on National Socialism, he was forced to leave his homeland when Hitler came to power. Now, he was teaching at Union Theological Seminary in New York. In his sermon, Tillich quoted the prophets Isaiah and Jeremiah, who were able to face the tragic defeat of their nation and still speak for God. Tillich said the prophets' power and insight sprang from the fact that they did not really speak of the foundations of the earth when they were shaken, they spoke of Him who laid the foundations, and who would shake the foundations. He said they did not speak of the doom of the nations as such; they spoke of Him who brings doom for the sake of His eternal justice and salvation. Tillich quoted Isaiah: **The foundations of the earth do shake. . . . Under the weight of its transgression earth falls down to rise no more! Lift up your eyes to heaven and look upon the earth beneath: For the heavens shall vanish away like smoke. And the earth shall grow old like a robe; The world itself shall crumble. But my righteousness shall be forever, And my salvation knows no end.** (24:18–20)

"God is the foundation upon which all foundations are laid, and this foundation cannot be shaken. There is something—immovable, unchangeable, unshakable, eternal—which becomes manifest in our passing and in the crumbling of our world. On the boundaries of the finite, the infinite becomes visible."[3]

So, what are you to do when your world shakes and trembles? The Lord says, **"stand up straight, lift up your heads, for your salvation is at hand."** I think that means to take courage and be alert to the things of God and to realize God is nearest when we need Him most. "On the boundaries of the finite, the infinite becomes visible." Sooner or later, every world is shaken. Your world is shaken and mine is shaken. We need to know what to do . . . how to find faith . . . how to find God.

Many of you know this already, for I have watched some of you stand tall and reach for God when your world collapsed. Only recently, I went to see a couple whom I had known but had not seen for many years. I remembered her courage when, as a young mother of two small children, her husband contracted tuberculosis and was hospitalized for ten months. She went to work to support the family. Now, after all these years, she had cancer. When I saw them, she was just as courageous as ever. After a surprisingly pleasant visit, I asked what I could do to help. She said simply, "Prayer would be good!" I prayed, of course, but more importantly, I realized she knew then what she had always known: when the foundations are shaken, your salvation is at hand.

Once again then, what do you do when everything begins to fall apart? You follow the admonition of our Lord: **"When these things begin to take place, stand up straight, lift up your heads, for your salvation is at hand."**

In the name of Christ, *Amen.*

NOTES
1   Whitman, Walt, Quicksand Years.
2   Howell, Elizabeth Lloyd, "Milton's Prayer of Patience."
3   Tillich, Paul, *The Shaking of the Foundations*, Charles Scribner's Sons, 1948,
    p. 9.

8.

The Foolishness of Preaching

I began preaching when I was in college, sixty-five years ago. Those early sermons were, for the most part, stories with very little depth. My preaching has been my education. It was the reason I went to college and seminary in the first place, and, through study and preparation, I have learned far more than any of my listeners. It has been exciting and humbling across the years to hear some of the great preachers: Wyatt Aiken Smart, E. Stanley Jones, W. E. Sangster, Leslie Weatherhead, Billy Graham, Martin Luther King, Jr., George Buttrick, Colin Morris, Kenneth Goodson, Carlyle Marney, Fred Craddock, Tony Campolo. I have read the sermons of so many others that I would like to have heard. One of the serious restrictions of preaching is that one has little opportunity to hear those who live in other places or those who love and serve God through other avenues of faith.

Preaching has changed during these more than sixty years. When some of the older preachers' sermons are read today they seem archaic in style, stiff and formal in presentation. The current preaching style is more personal, more informal, less literary, less structured. It is not better or worse, but perhaps it fits the time—as it should.

One Sunday nearly twenty years into my retirement from Dauphin Way, I preached again in that great church as Pastor Emeritus. I was eighty-one. On that occasion I decided to preach on "The Foolishness of Preaching":

For the word of the cross is folly to those who are perishing, but to us who are being saved it is the power of God. For it is written, "I will destroy the wisdom of the wise, and the cleverness of the clever I will thwart." Where is the wise man? Where is the scribe? Where is the debater of this age? Has not God made foolish the wisdom of the world? For since, in the wisdom of God, the world

did not know God through wisdom, it pleased God through
the folly of what we preach to save those who believe. For Jews
demand signs and Greeks seek wisdom, but we preach Christ
crucified, a stumbling block to Jews and folly to Gentiles, but to
those who are called, both Jews and Greeks, Christ the power of
God and the wisdom of God. For the foolishness of God is wiser
than men, and the weakness of God is stronger than men.

I CORINTHIANS 1:18–25 (RSV)

IT IS A GREAT joy to preach again, and a blessing to *be able to preach!* The first time I preached here was thirty-seven years ago. I served as Senior Minister at Dauphin Way for eighteen years, and for forty years I served as an active minister in the United Methodist Church. In May of this year, I will have been ordained fifty-seven years. I tell you all that so you won't think me presumptuous to speak today about "The Foolishness of Preaching."

Ministry is a multitude of things: administration, counseling, teaching, fund raising, motivation, visitation, leadership. But in our Protestant tradition, the minister is primarily the preacher. Bishop William A. Quayle said that preaching is not so much the art of making and delivering the sermon, as the art of making a preacher and delivering that.[1] Therefore, all of us preachers might say, in the words of Saint Paul: **"Now I would remind you, brethren, in what terms I preached to you the gospel, which you received, in which you stand, by which you are saved . . ."** (I Corinthians 15:1–2) That is, was there sincerity and integrity, was there steadfastness, compassion, and personal sacrifice in our proclamation of the Good News of Jesus Christ?

It has been my greatest satisfaction, my hardest work, and at times my complete frustration to stand in the pulpit and try to speak for God. From that lifetime experience, I know all too well the inadequacy of words, but I also know the adequacy of the Word of God. It was precisely that tension between human speech and the divine Word that caused Saint Paul to say: **"it pleased God by the foolishness of preaching to save them that believe."** (I Corinthians 1:21)

When I was first appointed to Dauphin Way, I was aware that preaching would be critical. This pulpit is elevated and lofty! In the main sanctuary there are seven steps leading to the pulpit. Biblically speaking, seven is the number of perfection. That number of steps is to remind the preacher that a sermon should be well prepared, well delivered, and consistent with the Word of God. A few years ago, when my granddaughter Rebecca was eight years old, I led her up these stairs and into this pulpit. I said, "Notice there are seven steps, to remind me to preach a perfect sermon." Without hesitation she said, "Seven steps are there to remind you of your seven perfect grandchildren!"

When I began my ministry at Dauphin Way and approached the elevated pulpit with its suspended soundboard, I did so with a certain fear and trembling. I was given to believe there was a secret lever hidden somewhere amidst the congregation, and should the sermon be either too long or too boring, the lever would be pulled, and the descending soundboard would snuff out the preacher! (I lived with an understandable anxiety throughout the years!)

Many years ago, Dr. Vernon Hunter, then Pastor of Springhill Presbyterian Church, visited me at Dauphin Way. When he looked at the raised pulpit he said, "That pulpit is ten feet above contradiction!" But it is not, nor should it be, because preaching is not only the glorious Word of God, it is also inglorious human speech.

Today we are skeptical of words. Because of mass communication—the media, the web, the blogs, email; TV and DVD; fax machines, telephones that talk or text or take pictures; because of iPods and Blackberrys that both twitter and tweet, there is a glut of words. We live in an information society. If anything, we have *too many* words.

Did you know the English language is constantly changing and enlarging? "At the turn of the century words were being added at the rate of about 1,000 a year. In 1989, the increase was reported to be 15,000 to 20,000 words a year. In 1987, the *Random Unabridged Dictionary* included over 50,000 words that had not existed twenty-one years earlier and 75,000 new definitions of old words."[2] To make the point, the *Merriam-Webster Dictionary* recently (2006) added the word "Google," as a verb!

Gamaliel Bradford has a book called *Damaged Souls*. It is about those discredited figures in American history like Benedict Arnold, Aaron Burr,

Benjamin Franklin Butler, and John Randolph. Bradford said the one thing these men had in common was an easy facility with speech. "The tongue was the most vivid and effective thing about them. They used it with singular, passionate urgency to forward their own purposes. . . ."[3] He said every one of them was a busy, active man to whom words were mere tools. That's all; no more. Just ready, handy, terrible tools! It is so tragic when words become manipulative and are used to sway mankind for selfish purposes.

No wonder we speak of "mere words" or refer to a person as "all talk." Remember Eliza Doolittle, in *My Fair Lady*. "Words, words, words. Don't tell me you love me, show me!" Today we are eager to experience the action of life, not its verbiage. Almost everyone agrees that the President Obama's recent address to the Joint Session of Congress was well crafted and well delivered, but if it is not followed by success it will be well forgotten.

We are skeptical of words, because words can seldom describe how we feel. The pain and the fear of life are expressed not so much by words as by a gasp or by a sigh or by shocked silence. Feelings are seldom expressed in accurate phrases. If the perfect description comes at all, it comes much later—when time has passed, the emotion is gone, the pain has softened, and we can be objective about the pain and the damaging hurt.

At best our words are imperfect signs. They point to something, to be sure, so we can reach agreement and common understanding, but they are imperfect signs to express the fullness of thought. Jonathan Swift, in *Gulliver's Travels*, recommended to diplomats going into a foreign country where they did not know the language, to take along all of the objects to which they might refer, then as the subject came up in conversation, they could simply point to that object. It is an obviously inadequate solution! We are skeptical of words!

So Christopher Morley commended silence:

> Quiet is what we need.
> By telephone, the press, the mail, the
> doorbell, radio, AP or NAM or CIO,
> We're micro-organized and overgrown
> With everybody's business but our own;

Pipe it down, chain talkers. Muffle and slow
the rapid pulse. I wonder if you know how
good it feels, sometimes to be alone?
Incessantly loquacious generation,
Let yeah and nyah be your communication.
Before the world comes open at the seams
Invest some private enterprise in dreams.
In unimpassioned silence we might find
(if ever) What the Author had in mind.[4]

But that is not the whole story. I can also testify to the *power* of words. We are still moved by the words of Shakespeare: "What a piece of work is man! How noble in reason! How infinite in faculties! In form and moving, how express and admirable! In action how like an angel! In apprehension, how like a god!"[5] We are motivated by quotations from Lincoln: "Now we are engaged in a great civil war, testing whether that nation, or any nation so conceived and so dedicated, can long endure"[6] or Churchill, or Roosevelt, or Martin Luther King, Jr. "I have a dream . . ." Read again the Declaration of Independence: "We hold these truths to be self evident, that all men are created equal. . . ." These are stirring words with lasting power and the ring of truth!

Emily Dickinson expressed it well:

A word is dead
When it is said,
Some say.
I say it just
Begins to live
That day.

Words do have lasting power; the Word of God lasts forever!

Philip Yancey said, "I became a writer, I believe, because of my own experience of the power of words. I saw that spoiled words, their original meaning wrung out, could be reclaimed. I saw that writing could penetrate into the crevices, bringing spiritual oxygen to people trapped in airtight boxes. I saw that when God conveyed to us the essence of his self-expression, God called it the Word."[7]

I can testify to the power of God's Word, not because I am a preacher—my own inadequacy would argue against me. It is the other way around: I can only be a preacher because of the power of the Word of God. Remember the text, **"it pleased God by the foolishness of preaching to save them that believe."** (I Cor. 1:21)

I love that line "the foolishness of preaching." To think that any human being, certainly one as limited as I, might try to speak for God is sheer foolishness. However, the better translation is **"through the foolishness of the message preached . . . it pleased God . . . to save them that believe."** It does sound like foolishness, this lesson for Lent. Saint Paul is referring to our salvation through the Cross of Christ. He is saying that in his time there were those who thought that if salvation came—not by miracles or divine power, but by one who was weak enough to be nailed to a cross—it was just foolishness. Or there were those who thought that if salvation could not be explained logically and philosophically it was certainly foolishness.

The same thought resonates today. Frederick Buechner put it like this; he said, "If the world is sane, then Jesus is mad as a hatter and the Last Supper is the Mad Tea Party. The world says, Mind your own business; and Jesus says, There is no such thing as your own business. The world says, Follow the wisest course and be a success; and Jesus says, Follow me and be crucified. The world says, Drive carefully—the life you save may be your own; and Jesus says, Whoever would save his life will lose it, and whoever loses his life for my sake will find it. The world says, Law and order; and Jesus says, Love. The world says, get; and Jesus says, give. In terms of the world's sanity, Jesus is crazy as a coot, and anybody who thinks he can follow him without being a little crazy too is laboring less under a cross than under a delusion."[8]

It is the foolishness of preaching! And yet, to you and me and to all who believe that Jesus was the Christ, to all who believe that God's own Son freely took our deserved place upon the cross—to all who believe *that*, the Cross of Christ is the power and the wisdom of God for our salvation.

When I think that Mark said, "**Jesus came . . . preaching,**" and Paul said, in Romans, "**faith comes by hearing, and hearing by the Word of God**" (Romans 10:17) I do not wonder that Luther said so bluntly, "Faith is an acoustical affair." It is, but it is a word you can see! "**The Word was made flesh . . .**" In *The Saint John's Bible*, the illuminated Bible from Saint John's Abby and University in Minnesota that many of us saw on display at the Mobile Museum of Art, the golden images of Christ are delicately mingled with the text, reminding us of that great word in Colossians (1:15) "**He is the visible image of the invisible God.**" He is a Word you can hear and *see!*

We know that human speech is not reliable, yet I assure you, the Word of the Lord is trustworthy and true. When Jesus Christ is the speaker, His audible words capture for us the infinite Word of God. Without the words of Jesus and the preaching of the Apostles and the witness of the scriptures, how would we know God's message, and how would we know God's Word?

It is so remarkable, as Karl Barth said, that God will reveal himself. Barth said "The fixed point from which all preaching starts is the fact that God has revealed himself. . . ." We do not hear the Word of God by our own wisdom, our own insight, our own perception! "God will make himself heard, he it is who speaks, not man."[9] When an ordinary person faithfully preaches the Word of God, those who listen may, but only by God's grace, hear the Living Word. We do not hear with our ears, we hear by the Word of God.

Dr. Carl Michalson was Professor of Systematic Theology at Drew University in New Jersey. He told of being absolutely astounded by the response of his three-year-old niece to an off-handed question. Her answer was profound. He had noticed her cute little nose, and he asked her, "Kristen, what do you smell with?" And she said, "A flower." He was amazed. He said the only person he knew who would give an answer like that was Martin Heidegger, the German existentialist. To probe a little further, he said, "Kristen, what do you run with?" She said, "My bicycle." What do you see with? "A mirror." He was so fascinated that he continued, "Kristen, what do you hear with?" She said, "A telephone."[10] But one day she may have the insight to answer, "I hear with the Word of God!"

"**Faith comes by hearing, and hearing by the word of God.**"

So it is true that some people will not believe unless the rest of us speak the sounds and live the life by which God's Word resonates upon the sensitivity of the world. As Saint Paul said, **"how shall they hear without a preacher?"** (Rom. 10:14) Every Christian is a preacher! Every Christian is a preacher; remember when you go out into the world to preach, *if all else fails*, use words!

The Word of God is creative; when God's Word is spoken an entirely new situation comes into being. As it is said in Pslam 33:6,9:

> By the word of the Lord the heavens were made,
> And all their host by the breath of his mouth . . .
> For he spoke and it came to be;
> He commanded, and it stood forth.

You can understand that from your own experience. When two young people are very much in love and sensitive to one another, and one of them says, "I love you," it is not a description of one's emotional experience, it is the creation of a new condition. Those lives are about to be changed. In the same way when we truly hear the Word of God saying, **"Believe on the Lord Jesus Christ and thou shalt be saved;"** a new condition is created.

Something changes when the Word of God is heard; the listeners do not merely *hear* about the Christ-event, they *become a part* of the Christ-event. The good news is heard upon the heart, and those who once were listeners become those who proclaim, by word and deed, the unsearchable riches of Christ! As Luther said, "Christ has made it possible for us . . . to be . . . his fellow priests."[11]

Here is the hard part. The Word of God requires a witness; it is that kind of word. Not every kind of word requires a witness, but the Word of God does. It requires that someone live in such a way that others can see the truth, and the grace, and the power of God's message.

Galileo discovered and verified that the sun does not move around the earth, but the earth moves around the sun. That violated the cosmology of the medieval Church. The Church said, "You must recant, and if you do not recant, you will be excommunicated and executed." Galileo recanted, says Carl Michalson, not because he was a coward, but because he knew his information was verifiable, scientific fact. Sooner or later that kind of information cannot be ignored; it will get around to everybody. You don't need to die for a scientific fact.[12] Galileo lived to be seventy-eight years old.

Certainly, there is also the kind of truth that can only exist if the witness is *faithful*. It is the truth of God's forgiveness, God's care for the outcast, and God's unconditional love.

An estimated 70 million Christians died for their faith over the past 2,000 years. More than half of these (45 million) died in the twentieth century. Thus, in a single century, more Christians lost their lives for reasons of conscience than in the previous 1,900 years. Christian witnesses, martyrs of the twentieth century, like Dietrich Bonhoeffer in Germany, 1945; May Hayman in New Guinea, 1942; Bishop Haik in Iran, 1994; Archbishop Luwum of Uganda, 1977; Rómulo Sauñe in Peru, 1992; and Bill Wallace in China, 1951 all paid the ultimate price for their faith. They represent unnamed millions who sacrificed their lives, not counting the cost of their witness for Christ.

Bill Wallace was a surgeon from Knoxville, Tennesee who was completely dedicated to Christ. He served as a medical missionary in China from 1935 to 1951 at the Stout Memorial Hospital in Wuchow. There he ministered throughout the Boxer Rebellion, the Japanese invasion during WWII, and the communist takeover following the war. During the Korean War, the anti-American feeling ran strong in China, and Dr. Wallace was urged to leave, but he said, "I will stay as long as I am able to serve." He was arrested by the Communists and accused of being a spy. He was tortured. He posted scripture verses on the wall of his cell to focus his faith. He was apparently beaten to death and his body deposited in an unmarked grave. However, faithful Chinese Christians did not allow that. Risking their lives, they found his body, laid him to rest in a proper service, and marked his grave with a sign that read: "For me to live is Christ."[13] Bill Wallace was a faithful witness to the Word.

Christian truth will only be known and the good news shared if those who profess Christ live like Christ and speak His Word. Spiritual truth cannot be analyzed or tested; it is only convincing when the witness is faithful. With that in mind, it has been a great privilege to know the faithful of this church and this community who through many years and many trials have been faithful to the Word of God.

In the name of Christ, *Amen.*

NOTES

1 Quayle, William A., Pastor-Preacher, The Methodist Book Concern, 1901.

2 Bryson, Bill, *The Mother Tongue*, Wm. Morrow, 1990, p. 151.

3 Bradford, Gamiliel, *Damaged Souls*, Houghton Mifflin, 1922, p. 13.

4 Morley, Christopher, Private Enterprise.

5 Shakespeare, William, *Hamlet, Prince of Denmark,*" Act II, Scene 2.

6 Lincoln, Abraham, Gettysburg Address.

7 Yancey, Phillip, *Finding God in Unexpected Places* Servant Publication, 1997, p. 47.

8 Frederick Buechner, *The Faces of Jesus*, Paraclete Press, 2006, p. 61.

9 Karl, Barth, *The Preaching of the Gospel*, Westminster Press, 1963, p. 17.

10 Michalson, Carl, *The Witness of Radical Faith*, Tidings, 1974, p. 80.

11 Luther, Martin, *Freedom of a Christian*, 1520.

12 Michalson, op. cit., p. 81.

13 Fletcher, Jesse, *Bill Wallace of China*, Broadman Press, 1963.

9.

Send My Roots Rain

By the mercy of God we are born into families and live in communities. The earthly family should be a foretaste of the family of God. Family love is one of humanity's greatest gifts, and the lack of it is an emptiness often remedied by the Church. In the rich fellowship of the Church it is comforting to know that familial love is provided for those alone and separated from their natural family. Growing out of our love for family there is within us a pressing desire to leave some heritage of value for those who follow after. Ruth and I have been uniquely blessed with four children and seven *perfect* grandchildren. (Seven is the biblical number for perfection.) On the Sunday I had the privilege of baptizing my youngest grandson, Ohan Missirian-Dill, I prayed and preached that God would "Send My Roots Rain":

> *That same day Jesus went out of the house and sat beside the lake.*
> *Such great crowds gathered around him that he got into a boat*
> *and sat there, while the whole crowd stood on the beach. And he*
> *told them many things in parables, saying: "Listen! A sower went*
> *out to sow. And as he sowed, some seeds fell on the path, and the*
> *birds came and ate them up. Other seeds fell on rocky ground,*
> *where they did not have much soil, and they sprang up quickly,*
> *since they had no depth of soil. But when the sun rose, they were*
> *scorched; and since they had no root, they withered away. Other*
> *seeds fell among thorns, and the thorns grew up and choked them.*
> *Other seeds fell on good soil and brought forth grain, some a*
> *hundredfold, some sixty, some thirty. Let anyone with ears listen!"*
> MATTHEW 13:1–9 (NIV)

DEEPLY ROOTED WITHIN OUR human nature there is a drive for worthwhile accomplishment, a desire to do something meaningful. It is important for us to know that our lives count, that there is a good reason for living and that we can make a difference. That is why we make New Year's resolutions; that is why every anniversary offers a new beginning. We are created in the image of the Creator. Our lives must have purpose. We are builders, schemers, doers.

There is an increasing body of evidence to show that children are born with an innate moral sense that, of course, must be developed and strengthened, but a distinction between right and wrong that is there from the beginning. The same transcendent moral principles are found among such diverse cultural groups as Greeks, Chinese, Indians, Hebrews, Anglo-Saxons, Babylonians, Norsemen, and ancient Egyptians. It is human nature to build up not to tear down, to accomplish not to destroy. "Pleasure soon exhausts us . . . but worthwhile endeavor never does."[1]

It is particularly true when you get a little older, and see life with a longer view—when you are able to look backward as well as forward—for it is then you search for the assurance of accomplishment. The desire to leave some lasting legacy engulfs us, absorbs us, particularly in those solemn and responsible moments like the birth or the baptism of a child. How intently we pray for every child offered into God's custody, that he or she may become "partakers of His righteousness and heirs of life eternal." Not only that the values we have lived for and the heritage we have honored will be continued into another generation, but that this child might be the one to offer humankind some signal contribution.

There is a beautiful moment in the Jewish tradition of circumcision. When the young boy is brought into the room the people say, "Blessed is he who comes!" for it is just possible that the Messiah has been born. Every child is precious. The potential of every child is limitless. We are optimistic about the future of every child, and we support the child, but we do so in the full knowledge that human achievement cannot succeed without God's guidance, for God Himself has placed within us the desire for accomplishment.

It is therefore very difficult to understand why so much of life is filled with disappointment. To make it worse, the disappointments may not be the consequence of any selfish or sinful behavior on our part. The disappointments occur, the hardships come, as if our garden had been infested with weeds—it's nobody's fault, we don't know why, we're not sure how. But somehow, the weeds are there, and they choke the good growth and block the energy that was meant for righteousness and peace.

In the spring or summer when you are working on the lawn, pulling weeds, it is a great time to consider one of the oldest theological questions of all: what is the nature of evil? Why do those troublesome and worthless plants grow so well? How do they flourish in such poor soil? How do they position themselves to take the available light and water? What is their purpose? Where do they come from? They thrive in all conditions choking out the good grass, requiring constant vigilance. They do seem to illustrate the mysterious presence of evil in our world.

Many years ago I received an anonymous letter. It described a mother's joy when her son was born, and the delight she took in rearing him. Then gradually, she began to tell of the alienation from her son, the many disappointments as he matured, the inevitable blaming of herself, the unwarranted guilt. It was a desperate prayer that all should not be lost. It was a prayer that this child might still grow into responsible manhood. I felt the hurt and pain:

> Oh, the sots and thralls of lust
> Do in spare hours more thrive than I that spend,
> Sir, life upon thy cause.

Those lines are from a poem by Gerard Manley Hopkins, a Jesuit priest of deepest faith and a sometimes-troubled nature. His poem is based on that question of Jeremiah, "Why does the way of the wicked prosper?" (12:1) Hopkins wrote:

> Thou are indeed just, Lord, if I contend
> With thee; but, sir, so what I plead is just.
> Why do sinners' ways prosper? and why must
> Disappointment all I endeavor end?

Wert thou my enemy, O thou my friend,
How wouldst thou worst, I wonder, than thou dost
Defeat, thwart me? Oh, the sots and thralls of lust
Do in spare hours more thrive than I that spend,
Sir, life upon thy cause. See, banks and brakes
Now, leaved how thick! laced they are again
With fretty chervil, look, and fresh wind shakes
Them; birds build—but not I build; no, but strain,
Time's eunuch, and not breed one work that wakes.
Mine, O thou lord of life, send my roots rain.[2]

It is a prayer known and used by every one of us. It a universal prayer, that life might come to something, count for something. "O thou Lord of life, send my roots rain." Do not let evil have its way. We have labored long and hard. Life has been a struggle. And now, O Lord, nourish our efforts; bring to perfection our good intentions. Let us know that we have made some lasting contribution, that it was all worthwhile. Send our roots rain.

Sometimes, when we feel useless, we can identify with Leonard Woolf, the husband of Virginia Woolf, the English author. He was a literary critic, a writer, an editor, and an economist. He edited all of his wife's novels. Reflecting upon his own life's work, he said this:

"I see clearly that I have achieved practically nothing. The world today and the history of the human anthill during the past fifty-seven years would be exactly the same as it is, if I had played ping-pong instead of sitting on committees and writing books and memoranda. I have therefore, to make a rather ignominious confession, that I must have, in a long life, ground through at least 150,000 to 200,000 hours of perfectly useless work."[3]

That's tragic, isn't it? And it does strike home with some of us. Our best causes and our finest intentions seem to bring forth so little fruit. "O thou Lord of life, send my roots rain."

Now let me give you this to remember: It was people who felt just that way to whom Jesus addressed the Parable of the Sower. His followers were filled with doubt! In the beginning they had been excited, and they had sacrificed to follow Him, but now they were discouraged. Things had not turned out at all as they expected. At first, they were convinced that He was everything—the wisest, the most wonderful—that He was the one who would redeem Israel, and they would be a part of that great religious revival!

But now, there was little success at which to point. The doors of the synagogues were being closed to Him; the religious leaders were now His bitterest enemies, seeking to destroy Him. (Mark 3:6) The crowds came not to hear Him, but only to see a miracle, and soon they went away and soon forgot. According to John's gospel (6:66) **"many of his disciples drew back and no longer went about with him."** Those who remained were discouraged, filled with anxiety, and the anxiety erupted into fear when He began to speak about His own death. Oh, how devastating that was, because their every hope was fixed on Him!

So it was to them, and to all of us still plagued by doubt, that Jesus told the Parable of the Sower. **"A sower went forth to sow . . ."** and some of the seed the birds devoured. Some, falling on rocky ground, sprung up quickly, but with no depth-of-soil were soon scorched and withered by the sun. And some fell among thorns that choked the growth. But none of that discouraged the sower in the parable. He sows the seed knowing that in spite of all the vicissitudes of life, the harvest is sure. It is guaranteed! In spite of adversity, the harvest will be abundant, the results far more beneficial than the sower ever expected—thirty-fold, sixty-fold, or even a hundred-fold. Thanks and praise be to God!

In answer to that ardent prayer, "O thou Lord of life, send my roots rain," God says: **"And I will send down the showers in their season; They shall be showers of blessing. And the trees of the field shall yield their fruit, and the earth shall yield its increase, and they shall be secure in their land; and they shall know that I am the Lord."** (Ezekiel 34:26–27)

I tell you, it is very important for every person of faith to know that the word of God cannot be defeated or abolished. It is important for you and me to know that there is no reason to be discouraged or downhearted—we trust the harvest to Him who is Lord of the harvest.

When the soil is prepared and the seed is sown, the farmer waits. That may be the hardest part of all, to wait—to wonder, to deal with doubts, to question the providence of God. It is easy to have faith when the spring comes:

As long as every April brings
The sweet rebirth of growing things . . .
Or when a primrose smiles at me,
Can I distrust Eternity?[4]

But in the hard cold winter, "the winter of our discontent," how laborious is the waiting. Then faith must remember that God appoints the harvest; it will come as He chooses. The time and place are His alone.

How true this was at the birth of Jesus. "So God prepared a time, and it seemed a godless time. God prepared a people, and they seem a faithless people. Yet at that time and through that people God did the unimaginable thing."[5]

Let me tell you about Henry Clay Morrison (1857–1942). He was the president of Asbury College and founder of Asbury Theological Seminary. William Jennings Bryan said, "He was the greatest pulpit orator on the entire American continent." H. C. Morrison had invitations from all across the country to preach. But very frequently in those days, when a Methodist presiding elder, the position that now we call a District Superintendent, learned that Morrison was coming to preach, he would cancel the service. Morrison was too enthusiastic, he spoke too much about holiness and sanctification. So Morrison preached a lot in camp meetings all across America.

One night, H. C. Morrison was in Baltimore, Maryland. He had confirmed invitations to preach in some of the largest churches in Baltimore, and only after he arrived did he find out that his meetings had been cancelled. There were no camp meetings at that time of year in Maryland, so Morrison had no place to preach.

Finally, a young minister approached him and said, "Brother Morrison, I have just a small little church, but we would love to have you come and preach. The presiding elder can't do anything to me, because I'm already on the bottom rung." So Morrison agreed, and he preached to a handful of people in Baltimore that night. At the close of the service, a 14-year-old boy came down to the altar to give his life to Christ. Morrison went down and knelt down next to him, and said, "Young man, what's your name?" He said, "E. Stanley Jones."

E. Stanley Jones became one the greatest Christian missionaries and Christian authors of the twentieth century. He received the Gandhi Peace Award from India and was nominated for the Nobel Peace Prize. Dr. Martin Luther King Jr. said that Jones' biography of Gandhi inspired him to nonviolence in the Civil Rights Movement.[6]

God is always doing the strangest things! He is working His will in unexpected ways, bringing about His unlikely harvest. It is not only true of the good causes you and I have labored for, and the loved ones we have prayed for, it is true for us personally. If we have been waiting for the evidence of spring—the confirmation of accomplishment, the harvest of benevolence when that confirmation comes—when we do receive the assurance from God that our labors have brought forth fruit, it will be like nourishing rain to a living seed. We will be transformed, as if the bondage were broken! It will be like a green shoot splitting through its shell upward through the earth flourishing in the sunlight. Our lives will thrive in the brightness, the refreshment, the nourishment that comes from God. Remember, we can become profitable servants at any time at any age. **"Ye that have ears to hear, let him hear."**

Ruth and I moved to Mobile in 1953, the first year of our marriage. We lived in Merrimack Apartments. Our small apartment was newly furnished, sparse but comfortable. The item I remember most clearly was a housewarming gift from a friend. It was a luxuriant Dutch amaryllis. Tall and stately, brightly colored, it provided a radiant centerpiece for our home. I remember yet the rich red color against the light-green wall.

At the end of summer, when the dormant season came, we carefully placed the bulb into the cool darkness, as we understood we should, to await the next planting time. By early spring we had forgotten all about the bulb and failed to plant it. Months later we accidentally opened that remote closet, and there it was—blooming! Blooming! We could not believe it. Weak and pale was its bloom, but strong and courageous was its growth. Without any soil, without any water, without any light, it grew and it blossomed.

Let me say to you, God does not neglect His children. We will not be left without comfort, without guidance, or without love. If a poor, earthly amaryllis can bloom alone, how much more will God the Father send the harvest to His own! Yes, pray earnestly for all those you love and have labored for: "O thou Lord of life, send my roots rain," but be assured of this, that you are speaking to the Father of Our Lord Jesus who said, **"A sower went forth to sow . . . and . . . seeds fell on good soil and brought forth grain, some a hundredfold."** Oh yes, "Thanks be to God who gives us the victory!"

In the name of Christ, *Amen.*

NOTES

1   Richter, Jean Paul.
2   Hopkins, Gerard Manley, "Thou Art Indeed Just, Lord."
3   Woolf, Leonard, "The Journey Not the Arrival Matters," Hogarth Press, 1969, p. 157.
4   Hay, S. H., "Prayer in April."
5   White, Reginald E. O, *The Stranger of Galilee*, Wm. B. Eerdmans Pub. Co., p. 14.
6   As told to Dr. Jones' daughter, Eunice Jones Mathews.

10.

The Hour of Knowing

Protestants have always been people of the Word, believing the Holy Scripture contains all things necessary for salvation, and whatever is not contained in scripture or cannot be proved by the scripture is not required as an article of faith. We read the Word and preach the Word as a means of coming to faith in Jesus Christ who is Himself the true and living Word of God. That is not to say the Sacrament of the Lord's Supper may be neglected; it certainly may not. The Lord's Supper is a means of grace through which God works in us to initiate, strengthen, and confirm our faith. In our tradition the Wesleyan Revival was not only an evangelistic revival, but also a sacramental revival. Consequently, the Holy Communion was offered every Sunday at Dauphin Way in one of the services and in every service the Holy Communion was offered at least once a month. The Holy Eucharist or The Great Thanksgiving should be one of the most moving and meaningful moments of Christian worship. I wanted to be sure our congregation understood the deep significance of Communion, so, on the first Sunday of June 2010, I preached "The Hour of Knowing":

> *As he came near and saw the city, he wept over it, saying, "If you,*
> *even you, had only recognized on this day the things that make*
> *for peace! But now they are hidden from your eyes. Indeed, the*
> *days will come upon you, when your enemies will set up ramparts*
> *around you and surround you, and hem you in on every side.*
> *They will crush you to the ground, you and your children within*
> *you, and they will not leave within you one stone upon another;*

because you did not recognize the time of your visitation from
God."

LUKE 19:41–44 (NIV)

RUPERT BROOKE, THE YOUNG English poet, dead at twenty-eight, representing the idealism that died with WWI, has a poem called "The Voice," which, to me is memorable for one line, and for what that one line suggests:

> Safe in the magic of my woods
> I lay, and watched the dying of the light.
> Faint in the pale high solitudes,
> And washed with rain and veiled by night,
>
> Silver and blue and green were showing.
> And the dark woods grew darker still;
> And birds were hushed: and peace was growing;
> And quietness crept up the hill.
>
> And no wind was blowing—and I knew
> That this was the hour of knowing.[1]

"The hour of knowing" is a memorable phrase! There is an "hour of knowing" that sometimes comes to us with such clarity that we know the truth, or we know our calling, or, after some indecision, we know clearly what we must do. It is also a tragic time when the hour of knowing passes, and there is no change, nothing accomplished, nothing done.

The hour of knowing applies on many levels. Hopefully, the tragic oil spill in the Gulf of Mexico has provided an hour of knowing, that the many smaller spills have not. We should know by now that the good earth is fragile, and we Christians are required to be good stewards of God's created world. We should know by now that the love of money is a powerful incentive, and that the production of energy, just like the world of commerce, must be regulated and protected from the appetites of greed. Long ago, but certainly by now, America should have reached the hour of knowing regarding the necessity of producing renewable energy. We are all to blame. But on behalf of those ordinary persons, those of low to moderate income whose livelihood depends on the seafood industry, tourism, and recreation, I hope we have not lost the hour of knowing. I hope it is not too late to protect the environment and build a clean, safe, and productive world and put in place the safety codes to make sure this never happens again.

Sometimes with young people there comes an hour of knowing . . . a moment of maturity, the realization that they must be responsible, the awareness that someone else is depending on them; not always the other way around. It is a realization that everybody sacrifices, that either we get what we want now and pay for it later, or we pay for it first and get it later. Either way, everybody sacrifices.

In religion, too, there is an hour of knowing, a dawning of certainty: a rarified, clear, and convincing moment that often changes our mind-set and redirects our energy. When that happens, we live holding on to that moment, and, regardless of the encircling gloom, we are no longer overwhelmed by doubt. We know what we believe and how we must act.

Leslie Weatherhead, the English clergyman, was traveling in Nepal and finally saw Mount Everest. He put it this way: "Once after a week of cloud and rain, I saw Everest at sunrise, and though the clouds returned, the certainty remained. I knew it was there!"[2] It was an hour of knowing.

The hour of knowing may be a time when we correct our perspective, or a time when we become aware that we have totally ignored another's feelings, and we must make amends. It may arrive as the result of suffering, or it may come like a deep, refreshing breath of air following an emotional struggle to live and breathe. In the hour of knowing, one comes to know that to truly live we must live and flourish in God's atmosphere of truth and love.

The hour of knowing may herald a new beginning for which we have long waited. Think, for instance, of Jesus, tied to the carpenter's shop for many years. Joseph had probably died, and Jesus, the elder brother, had to wait until the younger children came of age before He could begin His career. As He pointed out to His mother, His hour had not yet come. But finally, God's moment came. Jesus knew it was time to convey the message that burned within His breast. It was *the hour of knowing*!

The deepest question is: Can we know God? Can we gain some insight to the purpose of existence? Can we be certain that in prayer, in worship, in the Bible, at the Holy Table, we have fellowship with the Ruler of the universe? Can we know this is the time for us to live and act in His behalf?

That knowledgeable claim is staggering, yet there are millions who answer "yes." There are multitudes who are so sure of God that when calamity overtakes them, they are still unshaken and confidently assert that "the one above, in perfect wisdom and perfect love, is working for the best."[3]

I know it is not easy for everyone. For some strange reason, there are those who shut themselves away from the experience of knowing God—like a person deliberately stumbling with closed eyes through the wonder and the rapture of the world of light. But mostly, those without faith have just not been aware that the power of God is available.

There are those who refuse to know God, craving material proof. But that's illogical. We know material things by our material senses, but values—and God Himself—come to us in a different way. If you wish to see the stars, you will need good sight and a good telescope. A material object is known by material means. So, how do we see God? How do we arrive at the hour of knowing?

William Sangster said in order to know God we need silence—a great deal of silence. He said we need a quiet and unaccusing conscience; we need faith enough to wait until God moves to us. We need a willingness to be taught by those whose quality of living gives support to their claim. He said that in order to know God, we need an intelligent study of the Book that has fed the souls of millions, and we need a most special attention to the person and appeal of Christ himself.

Knowing doesn't come without effort. The only way to anticipate the hour of knowing is to plan for it expectantly, to make things ready. There is a marvelous story in the Old Testament of Abraham who sends an old servant back to the land of his people to find a wife for Isaac. It is a delicate task. Though it sounds like a romance novel, the future of Israel depends on it, and when it is successfully concluded, the old servant prays, "**I being in the way, the Lord led me.**" (Genesis 24:27) God cannot lead us without our being in the way! So do not be discouraged or impatient, but place yourself in the way for God to come to you and to know you. It may take time, but could time be put to better use?

Let me point out the importance of knowing Jesus if you would know God. Jesus said, "**Learn of me.**" He said, "**If you have seen me you have seen the Father.**" Nels Ferré, author, theologian, and teacher at Vanderbilt, was the child of Swedish parents who could not afford to educate their children. A childless aunt and uncle in the U. S. offered, when Nels was 13, to raise him as their own and give him a good education. His parents accepted the offer. It was a wrenching experience to go to live with virtual strangers in such a different place. He didn't know if he would ever see his family again. Nels was close to his mother and longed for some word from her that would sustain him through the time to come. There was only silence throughout the day before he was to leave. Silence through supper. Finally he went to bed and cried himself to sleep. In the morning, during breakfast, she did not speak a word; in the cart to the village, no word. Finally he boarded the train. As the train moved out of the station, his last glimpse of her was one he never forgot. With tears streaming down her cheeks, she held a scrawled note for him to read: "Remember Jesus most of all." It was an hour of knowing. It molded his life.

That final meal with Jesus on the night He was betrayed, the Last Supper, was for the disciples the hour of knowing. It had been a trying week for Jesus in an angry city. His friends had urged Him not to go to Passover this year because His life was in danger! The crowds were restless. The leaders were plotting secretly and there were sinister rumors everywhere. Jesus' own disciples were in a touchy mood; the strain of it all was beginning to show. A quarrel broke out among them about which of them was the greatest . . .

Can you imagine it? Jesus, somber, weighted down with a burden no man ever had to carry and His faithful supporters, jealous, sullen, and sniping at one another. Then came this last night! He had but this one night left, one last chance to lay His divine commission upon the hearts of His followers.

So He arranged for the use of a room, an "upper room," a quiet place, guarded and secluded, where they would not be disturbed. Think about that room and notice that it was an upper room. It took them away from the street and above the mentality of street-level thinking. To ever be conducting the business of life, to always live on the level of the mundane is degrading to the human spirit. We need a place of quiet worship. Too often, as Wallace Hamilton puts it, "The din of the world's confusion is in our ears, the dust of it is on our shoes, the smell of it is in our clothes and the fog of its fuzzy thinking is in our minds." The place where we can worship God is our upper room.

When I was growing up, my father was fond of saying, "You can't keep the bluebirds from flying over your head, but you can keep them from building a nest in your hair." My father reported it was said by Dr. George Stewart, at First Methodist Church in Birmingham, and perhaps it was. I later saw it attributed to Martin Luther, and I suspect that in the sixteenth century, Martin Luther's time, it was already an old saying, But it is true, nonetheless.

We cannot help being exposed to the evils of this world, but we can keep from being preoccupied with evil thoughts. We have no way to protect ourselves or our children from the degrading values of modern culture. There is too much exposure, too much communication. There is no way to isolate ourselves. But we can provide an upper room for withdrawal and spiritual cleansing, a place for restoration, a place where we can re-establish the purpose of our lives. In such an upper room, we are not ashamed to ask our Lord for cleansing from the dust of the way. Remember how willingly, in the Upper Room, Jesus washed His disciples' feet.

That Holy Meal where Jesus washed His disciples' feet became for them an hour of knowing, when each disciple looked into his own soul. Jesus said, **"One of you will betray me."** (Matthew 26:21–22) And in that moment, they did not point to one another, but each one said, **"Is it I, Lord?"** God was revealing each disciple to himself. In John's account, Jesus rises from the table and washes His disciples' feet, and He says to them, **"You are clean, but . . . not every one of you."** (John 13:10)

In Dorothy Sayers's play "The King's Supper," Peter whispers to John, "John, why does he say that we are not all clean?" And John whispers back, "I do not know, Peter, but when I look into my heart, I find it full of unswept, dusty corners."[4]

Each one looked inward, frightened, lest he find
A shoddy place where he had dreamed of steel.
None placed the guilt on any other guest
Who had partaken of that gracious meal."
    —Helen Welshimer

During World War II, when the Nazis were raining death on England, Leslie Weatherhead, whose own church was destroyed in the blitz, said, "When I am hot and rebellious, bitter and cynical and sarcastic; when it seems that evil can win the world and the battle is to the strong; when it seems that pride possesses all the high places, and greatness belongs to those who can grab the most; when it seems that faith is mocked and humility is trodden in the dust; when pity seems weakness and sympathy folly; when a foul egotism rises up within me, bidding me assert myself, serve my own interest and look out for number one . . . then O my God, as I listen down the corridor of the years for the voice of the Almighty, may I hear the gentle splashing of water in a basin, and see the Son of God washing his disciples' feet."[5]

When the disciples gathered again in the Upper Room, after Calvary, brokenhearted, leaderless and seeking refuge, it was there He found them! And there they experienced the incredible joy of Jesus breaking through their barriers of faithlessness and misconception to reveal Himself as the risen Savior.

It was in that Upper Room, away from the world, that the disciples were able to see themselves as they actually were, where they learned to be servants, where the Lord Christ came to them in power. From then on the disciples knew, and now the whole Church knows, that Christ can wash us clean from the sins of the journey. From then on the disciples knew, and now the whole Church knows, that to follow Jesus we must be the servants of all.

Today, with this Holy Meal which we are about to partake, in this Upper Room where we wait and worship, let this be for us the hour of knowing, the moment when we recognize our own sinfulness, when we accept the cleansing of Christ, and when we behold the power and the presence of the risen Lord.

Let today be for us all, the hour of knowing.

In the name of Christ, *Amen.*

NOTES

1   Brooke, Rupert, "The Voice," *The Collected Poems of Rupert Brooke*, Dodd Mead & Co., 1915.

2   Weatherhead, Leslie.

3   Anstice, Joseph, "O Lord How Happy Should We Be," 1836.

4   Sayers, Dorothy L. *The Man Born to be King*, William B. Eerdmans, 1943, p. 237.

5   Weatherhead, Leslie.

11.

There Was Eden

Every sermon exposes the speaker to some degree; too much personal exposure is self-indulgent and too little is preaching without passion. Over a ministry of eighteen years the congregation at Dauphin Way came to know me very well, but I was never comfortable with too much self-revelation. In celebrating the Festival of the Christian Home I always had my own home in mind, but seldom used it as an illustration. In this Mother's Day sermon, though she is not mentioned, my wife, Ruth, was foremost in my mind. Her love was entirely unselfish. She gave me and gave the world four wonderful children, seven wondrous grandchildren, and there was never a moment when she was not concerned for the welfare of each one of us. I never told her, but I hope she knew that sermons like this were all about her, for where she was "There Was Eden":

> *This is my commandment, that you love one another as I have loved you. No one has greater love than this, to lay down one's life for one's friends. You are my friends if you do what I command you. I do not call you servants any longer, because the servant does not know what the master is doing; but I have called you friends, because I have made known to you everything that I have heard from my Father. You did not choose me but I chose you. And I appointed you to go and bear fruit, fruit that will last, so that the Father will give you whatever you ask him in my name. I am giving you these commands so that you may love one another.*
>
> JOHN 15:12–17 (NRSV)

STRICTLY SPEAKING, MOTHER'S DAY it is not a Christian celebration; I mean, it is not a day set aside in the calendar of the Christian year. But Mother's

Day in the Church is a wonderful celebration of the Christian home, and a beautiful recognition of the values found in Christian motherhood.

There is in Genesis that poignant verse appropriate for Mother's Day, **"The man called his wife Eve for she would become the mother of all the living."** (Genesis 3:20) Mark Twain, in his little book *Eve's Diary*, gives a marvelous compliment to womanhood. He pictures Adam standing over the grave of Eve. Adam's mind wanders back over their years together: the Garden of Eden, the desire for knowledge, the freedom of disobedience, the birth of their sons, the death of Abel, the years of toil. He thinks of Eve and all she meant to him: love, loyalty, family, companionship; and he says simply, "Wheresoever she was, *there* was Eden."[1] Eden was paradise; it was his love, his security, his satisfaction. Eden was the natural and unbroken fellowship between humanity and God. "Where she was, there was Eden."

Today is Mother's Day, and there is within us all a feeling that motherhood is, or should be, a fulfillment of such nurturing love that self worth, satisfaction, and the fundamentals of faith become fashioned within the child.

Father Capon, an Episcopal priest, in a delightful book, *Bed and Board*, said that Mother is the geographical center of the family. Her role is to "be there" for the family—not necessarily to *be in that place*, but *to be the place itself*, to be there for them. Then he said, "Children love fat mothers. For while any mother is a diagram of place, a picture of home, a fat one is clearer; she is more there." Father Capon offers this toast to mothers: "May your husbands find you slim and your children remember you fat,"[2] whether you are, or not.

Sam Levenson, used to say his mother was a psychologist, without actually knowing the word. He said, "When she wanted us to take a pill, she would throw it on the floor. We would eat anything off the floor."

John Robert Quinn says his mother was a philosopher:

> My mother who boasted of no degree
> Was tutored in philosophy.
> Five butter beans within a pod
> Were generosity from God.
> A young pear tree in bridal veil

Was beauty's triumph over the gale;
And every star that blinked on high
Was proof that body and breath put by,
No darkness was so vast, so deep,
But that the shepherd would find his sheep.

Mother is place and everything to the child. How wise she is! A boy was walking aimlessly around in the room, and his mother said, "What do you want?" He said, "Nothing." She said, "You will find it in the box where the candy was."

A man, riding on the subway, wrote an ode to his mother:

I rose and gave her my seat
I could not let her stand.
She made me think of Mother
With that strap held in her hand.

Or to put all that a better way: May they simply remember that where mother was, "there was Eden."

I think we need to ask the question, why does the Christian church honor motherhood? The answer is found first in the primacy of Christian love. In today's lesson Jesus said: **"This is my commandment, that you love one another as I have loved you."** The human family is the most direct embodiment of love. William Ernest Hocking referred to the family as "the natural context for a sacrament," meaning that it is by way of human love that divine love is most frequently discovered. That is a great truth firmly imbedded in the good news of the Incarnation: **"The Word was made flesh and dwelt among us."** When Jesus came, His name was *Emmanuel*, "God with us." When the will of God is done on earth, the Kingdom of God is at hand. When our human arrangements are what they should be, something divine is revealed. It is true in every conversion; there is always a realignment from the human to the divine encounter.

Since that is true, wouldn't you like to know more about Mary, the mother of Jesus? She is only mentioned a few times in the New Testament.

The silent years of the childhood of Jesus veiled not only the Son but the mother. We can only imagine some of the things she must have done. She would have nursed the infant Jesus, holding Him gently, praying for Him to have a long and happy life. She would have sung to Him, silly songs to make Him laugh and soft songs to make Him sleep. She and Joseph would have found joy in each new accomplishment of the child Jesus, and felt the thrill of knowing that He was God's dear Son as well as their own. With some fear and trembling, she would have wondered how and when the child would know His call of destiny, as every mother wonders. One mother paid this tribute to Mary:

> I may not count holy beads in prayer to her,
> Nor place a lighted candle before her figure in a shrine.
> Yet, sometimes on the road to motherhood,
> I see her face, and sometime feel her hand—touching mine.

Why does the church honor motherhood? Because, through motherhood, humanity shares the creative activity of God! Our greatest urge is the desire to create. We are made in the image of the Creator. Creativity is the impulse of the self to go out from itself, to have some other expression. It is not only found in our desire for children, but in the arts, architecture, government, science, the whole of civilized endeavor. Within a happy marriage, creativity extends beyond just having children. The partners are constantly recreating each other, enhancing the other's creative abilities. Each one is being fashioned into something different and more complete from what he or she could have been alone, reaching out for more accomplishment.

Why does the church honor motherhood? Motherhood reminds us of our responsibility for each other. "**Love one another,**" says Jesus. Christian marriage is "the acceptance by a man and a woman of a permanent and unshakable responsibility for the other's happiness and well-being." This unselfish responsibility for the other is the mature requirement for parenthood. It is only when that unselfish responsibility is established between husband and wife that we should say: "**Let the little children come unto us.**" Love's adventure leads us toward a greater love, a love beyond the two of us. There is a line in the nuptial prayer: "Give them such fulfillment of their mutual affection that they may reach out in love and concern for others."

In *The Brothers Karamazov*, Dostoyevsky describes Alyosha falling asleep and dreaming about the wedding at Cana of Galilee. It is a dream of indescribable joy. But when he awakes he does a curious thing. He throws himself down on the earth and embraces it; he vows to love the earth forever.[3] It is to remind us that marriage must be an ever-widening adventure of love. Parenthood is a willingness to be responsible and reach out for greater loves. Where is that better taught than in the Christian home?

The Christian church celebrates Mother's Day, because motherhood forms in us the realization that there is no final maturity or satisfaction in life until we have learned to love and be loved. A child is apparently born with as little ability to love as to read. Love must be learned in the most elementary school of life. We learn at home how to love and be loved.

John Baillie recalls a hospital for abandoned infants in India, and how for lack of a mother, many of the babies seemed to pine away and die, however well fed and attended. The nursing rule at that time was not to handle the babies unnecessarily, to let them lie in their cots with a minimum of interference; until one day, an Indian woman walked around the ward cuddling a baby in her arms, saying, "Why don't you let the nurses hold the babies, a baby must have love!"[4] Nothing can take the place of that physical communication, the maternal touch, epidermis against epidermis, and not for any purely physical reason, but because a baby must have love.

It is part of the reason why the Church believes in infant baptism; the baby must have grace in order to grow and become a Christian child. Through the faith and the love of the parents and the Church, the grace of God reaches the infant child. That is the beginning of the child's faith:

> The baby has no skies
> But Mother's eyes,
> Nor any God above
> But Mother's love.
> His angel sees the fathers face,
> But he the Mother's, full of grace;

And yet the heavenly kingdom is
Of such as this.[5]

This is not sentimentalism, but sacramental doctrine. A study of malad-
justed teenagers in Oklahoma was so revealing—these young people were
asked how long it had been since their parents told them they loved them.
Not a single one could ever remember having heard such a comment. Then
they interviewed the ten best adjusted, most outstanding youth, asking them
the same question. Without exception they answered, "this morning" or
"last night." Every one of them had been reassured by their parents within
the last few hours. It is such an easy step from the realization of parental
love to that of divine love. "Where she was, *there* was Eden."

We don't honor all mothers indiscriminately. Just to give birth without
giving supervision or guidance or love is not reason enough for Christian
celebration. It is a mother's responsible love we honor and cherish.

As William Cullen Bryant prayed:

All-gracious! grant to those who bear
A mother's charge, the strength and light
To guide the feet that own their care
In ways of Love and Truth and Right.[6]

Well, it's Mother's Day, a wonderful tradition, and we can easily understand why the Church praises godly mothers and celebrates the Christian
home. But we want to be sure to honor mothers with some thoughtful
understanding. It is not enough to give her a box of assorted chocolates
or a bottle of apple-blossom perfume, take her to lunch and let it go for
another year. So here is another question: What does Mother really want?

I believe that what she really wants is you, not just for one day in May,
but throughout the year! I believe what she wants is some regular communication, some feed-back, some listening, some sharing. She wants to
know *you* at each stage of your life and she wants you to know *her*: know
her as a person, know her feelings and emotions, her memories, and her
accomplishments. The Lord commanded that we love one another. Some-

time we must bring Eden to her; she who was once Eden to us. A mother wants to know you and wants you to know her as a person. And of course, a Christian mother wants you to be strong in the faith. She wants you to grow up spiritually and stake out a mature faith of your own.

You must forgive my old stories! Some of you may remember Anna B. French. She was a member of Dauphin Way for many years and for a while she served the church as Director of Food Services. She was a lovely, frail, delicate woman deeply dedicated to Dauphin Way and devoted to Christ. Under difficult circumstances she reared ten children in the church; her husband died some years before. But on Mother's Day in 1987, to her great surprise, all of her children and their families came to join her in worship. What a joy! When Anna B. came to worship there they were: children, grandchildren, great-grandchildren—all waiting for her. I never saw anyone more proud! There were forty-four all together; they took up four rows of pews. They knew this would be the one thing that would please their Christian mother most of all, to be together in worship. What a beautiful expression, what an unforgettable way to show their love and to say to her, "Because of your love, we found God's love," Where she was, there was Eden.

In 1952, when John Steinbeck wrote *East of Eden*, he was expressing the human need for understanding, for acceptance, and for God. The tragic story echoes the frequent tragedy of human choice. The title was based on a verse in Genesis (3:24) that describes the Fall of Man: **"and God cast Adam out to the east of the garden of Eden."**

East of Eden is a tragic story, both in the Bible and in Steinbeck's greatest novel. "East of Eden" is where humanity is no longer innocent, where intimacy with God is no longer possible, where toil and death become inevitable. Now here is the good news! As Christian believers, what was lost for us by the first Adam, was regained by Christ, the second Adam. Saint Paul put it this way: **"The first Adam became a living being; the last Adam became a life-giving spirit . . . Just as we have borne the image of the man of dust, we shall also bear the image of the man of heaven."**

In Christ, humanity regains its Paradise. Through faith in Him we enter into the eternal Kingdom of God's holy rule. It is the particular gift, responsibility, and joyful privilege of mothers to point their children to that holy Kingdom, until each child shall recognize, and claim as his own, citizenship in the Kingdom of God.

It is also true, that in those sad, sad times when parents fail their divine responsibility, that the church—the Mother Church, the brothers and sisters of Christ—must offer to "whosoever will" an invitation to be at home in the glorious Kingdom of God's dear Son. Only in such a way is Paradise *regained*!

In the name of Christ, *Amen*.

NOTES

1   Twain, Mark, *Eve's Diary*, Harper & Brothers, 1906, p. 109.
2   Capon, Robert F., *Bed and Board*, Simon & Shuster, 1970.
3   Dostoevsky, Fyodor, *The Brothers Karamazov*, Book VII, Ch. 4.
4   Baillie, John.
5   Tabb, John Banister, "An Idolator."
6   Bryant, William Cullen, "The Mother's Hymn," 1864.

12.

Beyond the First Range of Hills

O n Memorial Day, America commemorates the unmatchable gift of life given by men and women who died in the service of their country. It is a national day of remembrance, not, strictly speaking, a religious memorial. Yet, "their last full measure of devotion" has preserved our freedom, including freedom of religion. The church also has lost its heroes, and they must be remembered as well on Memorial Day or All Saints Day. I was ordained an elder in the Methodist Church fifty-eight years ago. Now, in my later years, I sometimes finger through the files of funeral homilies and remember those great friends and pillars of the church that have been a blessing to me, that have kept the faith, and have passed on the Good News to another generation. It has been pointedly observed that the Christian faith is only one generation away from extinction. One Memorial Sunday, I preached "Beyond the First Range of Hills":

> *Now faith is the assurance of things hoped for, the conviction of*
> *things not seen. Indeed, by faith our ancestors received approval.*
> *By faith we understand that the worlds were prepared by the*
> *word of God, so that what is seen was made from things that*
> *are not visible. By faith Abel offered to God a more acceptable*
> *sacrifice than Cain's. Through this he received approval as*
> *righteous, God himself giving approval to his gifts; he died, but*
> *through his faith he still speaks. By faith Enoch was taken so that*
> *he did not experience death; and "he was not found, because God*
> *had taken him." For it was attested before he was taken away*
> *that "he had pleased God." And without faith it is impossible to*
> *please God, for whoever would approach him must believe that*
> *he exists and that he rewards those who seek him. ⁷By faith Noah,*

97

warned by God about events as yet unseen, respected the warning
and built an ark to save his household; by this he condemned
the world and became an heir to the righteousness that is in
accordance with faith.

HEBREWS 11:1–7 (NRSV)

THIS IS MEMORIAL DAY weekend. For many people it is just the beginning of summer, but it is more than that. Memorial Day is a United States federal holiday observed on the last Monday of May, commemorating U. S. men and women who died while in the in the service of their country. U. S. service personnel are deployed today in Afghanistan, Iraq, and across the world, and all Americans are indebted to these courageous heroes for our freedom and for our way of life. We decorate our hearts and minds with prayer and praise in memory of those who made the ultimate sacrifice.

In fact, Memorial Day was formerly known as Decoration Day, enacted to honor Union soldiers of the American Civil War, and it was expanded after World War I. According to David Blight, Professor of History at Yale University,[1] the first Decoration Day was observed by former slaves in Charleston, South Carolina. A race track (Washington Race Course, today the location of Hampton Park) had been used as a temporary Confederate prison camp in 1865 as well as a mass grave for Union soldiers who died there. Immediately after the end of the war, the former slaves exhumed the bodies from the mass grave and re-interred them properly with individual burial places. They built a fence around the graveyard with an entrance archway and declared it a Union Cemetery. The work was completed in only ten days. On May 1, 1865, the Charleston newspaper reported that a crowd of up to ten thousand, mainly black residents, including 2,800 children, processed to the location for a celebration that included sermons, singing, and a picnic on the grounds, thereby creating the first Decoration Day.

Many of the southern states refused to celebrate Decoration Day due to a lingering hostility, but there was a notable exception in Columbus, Mississippi. On April 25, 1866, observing Decoration Day, Columbus, Mississippi commemorated both the Union and Confederate casualties buried in its cemetery.

The alternative name of "Memorial Day" was not commonly used until after World War II, and was not declared the official name of the holiday by federal law until 1967. The law changing Memorial Day from May 30th to the last Monday in May took effect at the federal level in 1970.

We in the Christian Church often observe Memorial Day not only in recognition of the heroes of freedom and democracy, but as an opportunity to look back across the years and honor the heroes of faith. It is a time to recount the stories of the soul and to reclaim the assurance of salvation.

Today I want us to remember the events and people who have brought us, as a church, to where we are today. I want us to "look back at tomorrow" with the assurance that what we remember, God *re*-members. God *re-orders* our history in such a way that it anticipates the magnificent future that He has in store for us. Memorial Day for the church is an occasion when our faith **"gives substance to our hopes and convinces us of realities we do not see."** (Heb.11:1 NEB)

Most people live entirely in the sensible, immediate moment, giving no further consideration to the journey of faith, but there are some who listen to the longing of the heart and reach out for God. Samuel Taylor Coleridge uses this analogy: "The first range of hills that encircles the scant vale of human life, is the horizon for the majority of its inhabitants . . . But in all ages there have been a few, who measuring and sounding the rivers of the vale at the feet of their furthest inaccessible falls have learned, that the sources must be far higher and far inward; a few, who even in the level streams have detected elements, which neither the vale itself nor the surrounding mountains contain or could supply."[2]

Christians are like that. Christians are people with the long view, who discover the meaning of existence beyond any literal representation, who live in a sacramental world knowing that the creation mirrors its Creator. Christians are those who believe that Jesus Christ is the way that leads "beyond the first range of hills." Our faith **"convinces us of realities we do not see."**

Throughout the Bible there are people of faith who see the deeper meaning of events. In the book of Genesis, when Joseph is reunited with his father, and his people who have been saved from starvation, Joseph's brothers,—who had betrayed him—come asking for forgiveness. Joseph forgives them saying, "**You meant it for evil; but God meant it for good . . .**" (Genesis 50:20) We could make that same remark about the Cross of Christ or about so many unfortunate circumstances in our own lives. Weakness and sin, selfishness and greed were meant for evil, but God's grace transformed it into good.

On Memorial Day in the church, as we remember the past and those whom we have lost, there may be some sadness still, some things unfinished, but more than anything, our backward glance will be a shout of victory for all those who have "**fought the good fight . . . finished the course . . . kept the faith.**" (II Timothy 4:7) "**These all died in faith, not having received what was promised, but having seen it and greeted it from afar, and having acknowledged that they were strangers and exiles on the earth**" (Hebrews 11:13)

Think for a moment how indebted we are to those heroes of faith who have gone before us and have given us the spiritual gifts necessary for our strength and guidance. We miss them all. We miss their personality, their wisdom, and their grace. We miss their quick readiness to support all good things. In our minds we still picture them, we quote them, converse with them, and consult with them. In the words of the poet:

> So much of what we live goes on inside—
> The diaries of grief, the tongue-tied aches
> Of unacknowledged love are no less real
> For having passed unsaid. What we conceal
> Is always more than what we dare confide.
> Think of the letters that we write our dead.[3]

Christians know that this life is always unfinished, that life doesn't make any sense unless the meaning of life lies beyond the first range of hills. Today, in some mysterious way, the Church Militant and the Church Triumphant are joined. There is a connection between this congregation and those who have gone before—between we "who see through a glass, darkly" and those who gaze upon the celestial city.

Saint Augustine wrote the *City of God* during the decline of the Roman

Empire. He called the church "that glorious and celestial city of God's faithful people which is seated partly in the course of these declining times . . . but chiefly in that solid estate of eternity."[4]

So it is with us. This church is seated in these difficult times, but chiefly in eternity. I know it is not easy—looking around at this building, these mortals here, hearing this poor preacher—to think that all this has to do with God. It is not easy to look beyond the first range of hills and see God's glorious and eternal Church.

C. S. Lewis in *The Screwtape Letters* pictured that contrast between the visible and the invisible Church. *The Screwtape Letters* are letters from Screwtape, a professional devil and undersecretary in the Department of Temptation, to his nephew, Wormwood, who is a junior tempter. In the second letter, Screwtape writes:

"My dear Wormwood, I note with grave displeasure that your patient has become a Christian. Do not indulge the hope that you will escape the usual penalties . . . In the meantime . . . There is no need to despair; hundreds of these adult converts have been reclaimed after a brief sojourn in the Enemy's camp . . . One of our great allies at present is the Church itself. I do not mean the Church as we see her spread out through all time and space and rooted in eternity, terrible as an army with banners. That, I confess, is a spectacle which makes our boldest tempters uneasy. But fortunately it is quite invisible to these humans . . . When he gets to his pew and looks around him he sees just that selection of his neighbors whom he has hitherto avoided. You want to lean pretty heavily on those neighbors. Make his mind flit to and fro between an expression like 'the body of Christ' and the actual faces in the next pew. It matters very little, of course, what kind of people that next pew really contains. You may know one of them to be a great warrior on the Enemy's side. No matter . . . Provided that any of those neighbors sing out of tune, or have boots that squeak, or double chins, or odd clothes, the patient will quiet easily believe that their religion must therefore be somehow ridiculous."[5]

Many times the Church looks ridiculous, because the ways of God are beyond human understanding. Faith in God must always make room for the mystery of the unexpected. **"How unsearchable are his judgments and**

how inscrutable his ways!" (Romans 11:33) I am amazed at the audacity with which some people speak of God, as if they know His mind, and there is no remaining mystery. When we are honest, the faith of most of us is that of the father of the epileptic boy: **"I believe, help my unbelief"** (Mark 9:24) Help me where faith falls short.

Henri Nouwen reminds us that three times in John's gospel doubting Thomas is identified by his other name, "Didymus," meaning "twin." The early church fathers commented that all of us are two people, a doubting one and a believing one. All of us need the support and love of a worshipping community to prevent our doubting person from becoming dominant and destroying our capacity for belief.

Hold on carefully to your capacity for belief. Faith is critical! It prevents cynicism, agnosticism and it opens the way to see beyond the first range of hills. If you are longing to understand God, let me remind you that belief comes first; faith precedes understanding. "I do not seek to understand so that I may believe, said Anselm, "but believe that I may understand."[6]

I myself, always wanted to begin with reason, with some kind of natural theology; I wanted to logically, step by step, uncover God. But I have come to realize that although human reason is important, alone it is not enough. The same reasonable facts can be interpreted differently; different people spin the truth in opposite directions.

> Two men look from behind prison bars,
> One sees mud, and the other stars.[7]

Therefore, to understand God we begin with faith. Is that so strange? We learn to speak before understanding the rules of grammar; we learn to walk before understanding the principles of balance. We start with faith. As the book of Hebrews says, faith **"gives substance to our hopes and convinces us of realities we do not see."** (Heb. 11:1) Great are those spiritual realities that lie beyond the first range of hills.

When you consider that faith is a matter of trust, when you hear the great saints of the Church tell the story of God's love, when you see beyond the first range of hills, it then becomes clear that in ways far ahead of our understanding God Himself comes to where we are and leads us home. **"For by grace you have been saved through faith . . . it is a gift of God"** (Ephesians 2:8)

Isn't that phenomenal: The Almighty God constantly seeks our companionship. Without rest, the Good Shepherd searches for His sheep! God in Christ comes to us and claims us in many different ways: To some, like Saint Paul, He comes with force and blinding suddenness. To others, as Schweitzer said, "He comes to us as One unknown, without a name, as of old, by the lake-side, He came to those men who knew Him not."[8]

Or as the Welsh poet, R. S. Thomas said, God came "as I had always known he would come, unannounced, remarkable merely for the absence of clamor."[9]

Think back across the years to the salient moments when God entered your life. God comes to us by many different avenues. He comes through tragedy and through joy, through music and worship and prayer, through criticism and conflict. He comes through study and thought and preaching. He comes quite often through the avenue of service to others. God comes through the family, and those who loved us; He comes through other members of the church. Sometimes it is inward and unexpressed, but when He comes we know that God has come to us to call us home.

Dennis Covington, who teaches creative writing at the University of Alabama at Birmingham, has written a fascinating book, *Salvation on Sand Mountain*. As a reporter, Mr. Covington covered the trial of a minister from Scottsboro, Alabama, who was convicted of using rattlesnakes, symbols of faith to him, in the attempted murder of his wife. Because of that assignment, Covington was drawn into the world of religious snake handlers. Throughout the assignment he remained an objective reporter, but he also became a part of that strange religious world. Unconsciously he was seeking his own roots, searching for his own identity, hoping to find his way home. (Aren't we all!) In the end he separated himself from that unusual community of faith, but through that experience he found himself, or more accurately, *God found him*.

In the last paragraph, a childhood experience provides this analogy of faith. Covington writes, "It is late afternoon at the lake . . . Most of the children in my neighborhood are called home for supper by their mothers. They open the back doors, wipe their hands on their aprons, and yell, 'Willie!' or 'Joe!' or 'Ray!' Either that or they use a bell, bolted to the doorframe and loud enough to start the dogs barking in the backyards all along the street. But I was always called home by my father, and he didn't do it the customary way. He walked down the alley all the way to the lake. If I was close, I could hear his shoes on the gravel before he came into sight. If I was far, I could see him across the surface of the waters, emerging out of the shadows and into the gray light. He would stand with his hands in the pocket of his windbreaker while he looked for me. This is how he got me to come home. He always came to the place where I was before he called my name."[10]

No matter where you are or what you are doing, the Almighty Father will come to where you are and call your name.

I know much of this world is discouraging. There is so much pain and trouble, so many problems and so few solutions. Dauphin Way Church will celebrate its centennial in 2013. The first building was a log cabin that had been torn down and reconstructed on the corner of Dauphin and Houston Streets. So much has happened since those pioneers began our church. "Through many dangers, toils, and snares, we have already come;" and through it all the church has glorified her Lord.

Cyprian was Bishop of Carthage in the middle of the third century. It was not a good time for the Church. Cyprian wrote to his friend Donatus, "This seems a cheerful world, Donatus, when I view it from my fair garden under the shadow of these vines. But, if I climbed some great mountain and looked out over wide lands, you know very well what I would see. Brigands on the high road, pirates on the seas . . . men murdered . . . under all roofs misery and selfishness. It is really a bad world, Donatus, Yet, in the midst of it I have found a quiet and holy people. They have discovered a joy that is a thousand times better than any pleasure of this sinful life. They are despised and persecuted, but they care not. They have overcome the world. These people, Donatus, are Christians."[11]

Let that define who we are, as a Church, as people of faith, as brothers and sisters in Christ. We are those who have overcome the world! We are

Christians who take the long view and see beyond the first range of hills. Our faith **"gives substance to our hopes and convinces us of realities we do not see."** (Hebrews 11:1) Thanks be to God for all that has gone before; thanks be to God for all that is yet to come!

In the name of Christ, *Amen.*

NOTES

1   Blight, David, director of the Gillder Lehrman Center for the Study of Slavery, *Resistance and Abolition*, Yale University, New York Times, May 29, 2011.

2   Coleridge, Samuel Taylor Biographia Literaria, William Pickering, 1847 p. 246.

3   Gioia, Dana Unsaid.

4   Saint Augustine, *City of God.*

5   Lewis, C. S., *The Screwtape Letters*, MacMillan Publishing Co., Inc. 1961, p. 11.

6   Anselm, Archbishop of Canterbury, 1093–1109, re-writing Augustine, Ten Homilies on the First Epistle of John.

7   Langbridge, Frederick.

8   Schweitzer, Albert, *The Quest of the Historical Jesus*, The MacMillan Co., 1957, p. 403.

9   Thomas, R. S., Suddenly.

10 Covington, Dennis, *Salvation on Sand Mountain*, Penguin Books, 1994, 239.

11 Cyprian, bishop of Carthage, writings, including letters, saved by the Church.

13.

Guide Me, O Thou Great Jehovah

Christians are bound by one supreme loyalty. We are called to be faithful to God through Jesus Christ, our Lord. This does not mean we do not have other loyalties. We are called as well to be faithful to our family, our friends and neighbors, and to our country. Yet it is because of our loyalty to God that we are strong and faithful in our less-demanding loyalties. I had this priority in mind when, on Independence Day, I preached, "Guide Me, O Thou Great Jehovah":

> Then the Pharisees went and took counsel how to entangle him in his talk. And they sent their disciples to him, along with the Herodians, saying, "Teacher, we know that you are true, and teach the way of God truthfully, and care for no man; for you do not regard the position of men. Tell us, then, what you think. Is it lawful to pay taxes to Caesar, or not?" But Jesus, aware of their malice, said, "Why put me to the test, you hypocrites? Show me the money for the tax." And they brought him a coin. And Jesus said to them, "Whose likeness and inscription is this?" They said, "Caesar's." Then he said to them, "Render therefore to Caesar the things that are Caesar's, and to God the things that are God's." When they heard it, they marveled; and they left him and went away.
>
> MATTHEW 22:15–22 (RSV)

ON INDEPENDENCE SUNDAY, THINKING of our supreme loyalty to God, I can imagine Jesus standing before the Pharisees and Herodians. He is looking down at the Roman coin which was used to pay the census tax. Then, raising His head to face His critics, Jesus says, "**Render unto Caesar the things that** are Caesar's, and unto God the things that are God's." (Matthew 22:21)

From the beginning, Americans have struggled to interpret that relationship between our faith and our national life, for the two stand in support of one another and at tension with each other. For as long as I can remember, I have thrilled to both the American dream and the call of Christ. As an American, I have been proud of our country and blessed to be a citizen. As a Christian, however, I have been uneasy about our failures and concerned about our future. As an American, I gladly pledge allegiance to our country, even though we have not fully achieved "liberty and justice for all." As a Christian, I pledge a deeper allegiance to God, which takes precedence over all other loyalties, because **"We must obey God rather than men."** (Acts 5:29)

Clearly seeing that support and tension between faith and country, our forefathers hammered out this new nation, creating a porous wall between government and religion. This porous wall would permit an interaction between the two without allowing either to control the other. This separation between church and state was a remarkable achievement. Some of the world's worst tyranny has been in nations ruled by religion. Equally oppressive has been the attempt of the state to control or destroy personal freedom and personal faith.

We are not a perfect society, but more than most, we are conscious that some things belong to God. Lincoln called America God's "almost-chosen people."[1] That qualification saves us from presumptuous pride or self-righteousness. Lincoln used the term when he was speaking to the New Jersey State Senate in 1861. He was on the way to his first inauguration. He said that even as a boy he had been impressed that the Founding Fathers had been struggling for something even more than national independence. They believed they were working for something that held out great promise for all the people of the world, for all time to come. Lincoln expressed his hope that this original idea would continue to direct the life of the country . . . and that he himself might be a humble instrument in the hands of the Almighty and of this, "His almost chosen people."

It is a curious phrase, "His almost chosen people." Did Lincoln mean that the secession crisis might overturn the good fortune that God had granted us? Did he mean that we *could* be the chosen people depending on the path we took? We are certainly not the chosen people if you mean by that more favored by God above other people or more loved and protected by God above other people. But I do believe we have been chosen for a unique opportunity under God to encourage peace and to foster individual freedom and human rights.

Let me remind you that America began with a clear sense of divine destiny: God leading the founders through their own kind of wilderness. Governor William Bradford, an eyewitness, reported how the *Mayflower* passengers landed on the American shore in mid-November 1620:

"They fell upon their knees and blessed the God of heaven, who had brought them over the vast and furious ocean, and delivered them from all the perils and miseries thereof . . . they had now no friends to welcome them, nor inns to entertain or refresh their weather-beaten bodies, no houses or much less towns to repair to . . . And for the season it was winter, and they that know the winters of that country know them to be sharp and violent, and subject to cruel and fierce storms, dangerous to travel to known places, much more to search an unknown coast. Besides, what could they see but a hideous and desolate wilderness . . ."[2]

The Puritans remembered the Hebrew people wandering in the wilderness and compared their own experience to that of the Israelites. The Atlantic Ocean would be their Red Sea, and they would consider themselves "New Israel," bound for the Promised Land. They would have identified with the majestic Welsh hymn:

> Guide me, O thou great Jehovah,
> Pilgrim through this barren land.
> I am weak, but thou art mighty;
> Hold me with thy powerful hand.[3]

When the Puritan ships reached Boston Harbor in 1630, John Winthrop, preacher and leader of the colony, delivered a sermon aboard the lead ship, *Arbella*. The title was "A New Model for Christian Charity." He sought to establish a Christian basis for the new civilization. It would follow the principles of the Sermon on the Mount: the strong would bear the weak, and the rich relieve the necessities of the poor. The new society would be a "city set on a hill," not a retreat from the world, but an example to the world. (From this, Beacon Hill in Boston took its name.) Winthrop's sermon, and the popular belief it expressed has been the keynote of American history. America has come to think of itself as a "city set on a hill," a beacon for mankind.

Herman Melville said, "We Americans are the peculiar chosen people, the Israel of our time . . . the political Messiah has come in us."[4] Reinhold Niebuhr pointed out that "We came into existence with the sense of being a 'separated nation' which God was using to make a new beginning for mankind. Our forefathers believed that we had been called out by God to create a new humanity. We were God's American Israel."[5] **Guide us, O Thou Great Jehovah!**

It would be tragic if America ever lost its dream. The American dream means more than prosperity, two cars, a college education, and a swimming pool. It has to do with our national destiny. Over and over again, that religious concept emerges in our national life. It is sometimes faint and overshadowed, but that main theme is still evident: America has a mission; America is called by God to be an example to the world. Notice how we have tried to think of all our wars as Holy Wars—to establish liberty, to ensure unity and end slavery, to make the world safe for democracy, to free the world from tyranny or communism, to prohibit aggression, prevent ethnic cleansing, and now to defeat terrorism and protect America. In these recent years we have continued to pray that our wars are just, and our men and women in the military will be free from harm.

Woodrow Wilson said, "America has the infinite privilege of fulfilling her destiny and saving the world."[6] Richard Nixon, bidding farewell to his staff on the morning following his resignation, said, "Without our leadership the world will know nothing but war, possible starvation and worse in the years ahead. With our leadership it will know peace and plenty."[7] I pray that with God's help we can offer our people, and the world, an enlightened and unselfish leadership that will lead to worldwide peace and prosperity. **Guide us, O Thou Great Jehovah!**

When Martin Luther King, Jr. was assassinated—one of three assassinations of major national figures in five years—the newspaper ran a cartoon showing a young black man with a grief-stricken face. He was saying: "Seems like every time I have a dream, I'm awakened by the sound of a gun. And, man, I'm fast running out of dreams." Langston Hughes wrote:

> What happens to a dream deferred?
> Does it dry up
> like a raisin in the sun?
> Or fester like a sore—
> and then run.
>
> Does it stink like rotten meat?
> Or crust and sugar over—
> like a syrupy sweet?
>
> Maybe it just sags
> like a heavy load.
>
> Or does it explode?

To be sure, there have been sad chapters in our history—times when we have forgotten our destiny, refused to share our dream, or proclaimed our religious piety as a protective cover for our prejudice and fear. There have been times when we should have prayed with President Lincoln "that this nation under God might have a new birth of freedom." Certainly, it would be a mistake to think that America was settled without any motive save religious liberty. Immigrants came to America seeking a haven from oppression and a doorway to prosperity. The national interest, the personal economy, the individual welfare have always been legitimate concerns for the American dream.

I was so naïve in my early years, unaware of the injustice around me, unconscious of a dream unequally shared. I was unsuspecting of the corruption; unable to see the hypocrisy behind much of the political oratory, unconvinced that leaders had clay feet. It is sobering to mature and to watch your dream begin to tarnish. Still, in spite of all the failures, there is what James Russell Lowell called America's Gospel:

> Our Country hath a gospel of her own
> To preach and practice before all the world—
> The freedom and the divinity of man,
> The glorious claims of human brotherhood
> And the soul's fealty to none but God.

I think it fitting, on Independence Sunday, to be reminded that one purpose of the Church is to be the conscience of the nation. There should be times when the Church speaks with the voice of the ancient prophets: "Thus saith the Lord!" Years ago, I heard President Eisenhower speak to the World Council of Churches in Evanston, Illinois. He said, "We hope you will touch our imagination, remind us again of the vision without which the people perish. Give us criticism in the light of religious ideals. Kindle anew in us a desire to strive for moral greatness and . . . show us where we fall short. We shall listen if you speak to us as the prophets spoke in the days of old."[8]

In Germany, after the atrocities of World War II, the Jews told the story that once there was a small but prosperous kingdom. The grain crop that year was abundant and the people rejoiced. But a prophet among them came to the king with terrible news. "Your Majesty, the whole harvest this year has been poisoned; anyone who eats it will go mad. It is your duty to destroy the harvest if the people are to survive." The king was stunned and asked for a day to consider the matter.

The next day he called the prophet and said, "This is my decision. We shall store this year's harvest in one place and what is left of last year's in another. You will eat of last year's harvest. My people and I will eat of the contaminated crop. However, it will be your duty, when you see any of us move away from sanity—when you see us become irrational, doing things we ought not to do—it will be your solemn duty to call to us and honestly say to us: 'You are mad! You are mad!'"

Sometimes it seems like the world has eaten poisoned grain. In chaotic times, times like these, with war, economic depression, natural disaster, educational disparity, moral depravity, the Church must cry out for the leadership of God and the principles of Christ. I believe the heart of democracy is set forth in New Testament principles: each individual has dignity and infinite worth in the sight of God; spiritually speaking, we are all equal; freedom of conscience is a divinely given right; we are our brother's keeper; we render unto Caesar the things that are Caesar's, but to God the things that are God's. **Guide us, O Thou Great Jehovah!**

Only in reliance upon The Almighty will civilized society and individual freedom survive. If there is any truth in America's destiny to save the world, or any hope in America's dream at home, then the Church must follow in the way of Christ and say clearly to the nation and the world, "This is the way that leads to life!"

It appears to me that when this country was founded, the affairs of state were guided by an array of talent and genius unmatched in history. But it is also notable that the men who framed the Constitution might not be called highly educated by today's standards. There was not a professor of government among them. Benjamin Franklin had only three years of formal schooling. George Washington was tutored in Latin until he was fourteen and later taught himself mathematics.

Bernard Baruch, financier, advisor to three presidents, expressed his belief "that most of the men who drafted the Constitution could not have met the entrance requirements for college." But he went on to say they "were well educated in the true meaning of the term . . . they knew how to think . . . they had learned how to blend living experience with the lessons of history . . . [and] they were deeply imbued with moral values. Their minds drew a clear distinction between good and evil, between principle and expediency. They were not uncertain about the values they believed in and were determined to uphold."[9]

I believe these remarkable men were led of God and committed to bring forth "a new nation conceived in liberty." George Mason, who helped draft the Constitution, looked back on those events and said, "we seemed to have been treading on enchanted ground."[10]

At one tense moment, when the constitutional debates seemed ready to break down, Benjamin Franklin took the floor. He said, "I have lived, Sir, a long time and the longer I live, the more convincing proofs I see of this truth—that God governs in the affairs of men. And if a sparrow cannot fall to the ground without his notice, is it probable that an empire can rise without his aid? 'except the Lord build the House they labor in vain that build it.'

Franklin continued, "I therefore beg leave to move that henceforth prayers imploring the assistance of Heaven, and its blessings on our deliberations be held in this Assembly every morning before we proceed to business."[11] It is so true that we cannot lead if we do not follow.

In Genesis (24:10–27 KJV) there is a beautiful, sensitive story of Eliezer of Damascus, the faithful servant of Abraham. He is entrusted with the delicate task of returning to Mesopotamia and selecting a wife for his young master, Isaac. The story is romantic, but romance was of no concern to Eliezer. At issue was the purity and preservation of the faith of Israel. Isaac must not marry a daughter of the Canaanites!

The old servant faithfully worked out a plan with God. When he reached the town of Nahor he made his camels kneel down outside the city by the well. It was evening, and the women came to draw water. The plan was this: When he said to a woman, "Pray draw water that I may drink," if she said, "Drink, and I will draw water for your camels also," she would be the one God had appointed for Isaac.

Rebecca came. She was lovely and not betrothed. When the stranger asked for water, she was gracious to share. Then she said, "I will draw water for your camels also until they have done drinking." The old servant gazed at her in silence, amazed. It is a beautiful story! Eliezer was invited to meet the family, and he shared the purpose of his journey. The parents said this must be a plan from God. Rebecca said she would go to be the wife of Isaac.

When that diplomatic task was successfully concluded, Eliezer prayed an unforgettable prayer: **"Blessed be the Lord God of my master Abraham, who has not left destitute my master of his mercy and truth: I being in the way, the Lord led me to the house of my master's brethren."**

It is a simple, magnificent prayer! **"I being in the way, the Lord led me . . ."** This is the message we need for our country and for ourselves. God cannot lead us through today's wilderness, nor fulfill our destiny, nor turn our dreams into actuality unless we follow in His way. " **I being in the way, the Lord led me . . .**" For our own happiness and redemption, we must be "in the way." For the peace and prosperity of our nation and for the world, we must be "in the way." For those of us who follow the Master, that means to be "in Christ" who said, "**I am the way . . .**" (John 14:6) and who said, "**Narrow is the way that leads to life.**" (Matt. 7:14)

So here we are, celebrating American Independence after two hundred thirty-four years. Here we are, early in the third millennium of the Christian Era. What more noble gift can each of us offer the nation and the world than to draw near to our God and walk from henceforth in His holy ways, with this as our prayer:

I being in the Way, guide me, O thou great Jehovah. I'm a pilgrim in this barren land. I am weak, but Thou art mighty. Hold me . . . hold us all—hold our church . . . hold our nation—with Thy powerful hand.

In the name of Christ, *Amen.*

NOTES

1   Lincoln, Abraham, *The Collected Works of Abraham Lincoln*, Vol. 4, ed. Roy P. Basler, Rutgers University Press, 1953.

2   Boorstin, Daniel J., *The Americans: The Colonial Experience*, Random House, 1958.

3   Williams, William, 1745.

4   Melville, Herman, *White Jacket*, Richard Bentley, 1850, p. 239.

5   Niebuhr, Reinhold, *The Irony of American History*, Charles Scribner's Sons, 1952, p.24.

6   Quoted in New York Times article by Jackson Lears, 3/11/03.

7   Quoted in New York Times article, 8/10/74.

8   Eisenhower, Dwight D., speech archived in "Records Pertaining to the Second Assembly of the World Council of Churches," Northwestern University Library, Box 3.

9   Baruch, Bernard.

10   Broadwater, Jeff, *George Mason: Forgotten Founder*, University of North Carolina Press, 2006, p. 107.

11   Lossing, Benson J., *Our Country, a Household History for All Readers*, 1877.

14.

The Tenth Leper

Not fear but gratitude is at the heart of the Christian faith—gratitude for God's great love, gratitude for the gift of God's only Son, gratitude for God's healing and mending grace, gratitude for life and love and life everlasting. Consequently, when the Day of National Thanksgiving arrives, it seems appropriate for the Church to endorse the theme and speak of thanksgiving to God. So I preached "The Tenth Leper":

> *On the way to Jerusalem Jesus was going through the region between Samaria and Galilee. As he entered a village, ten lepers approached him. Keeping their distance, they called out, saying, "Jesus, Master, have mercy on us!" When he saw them, he said to them, "Go and show yourselves to the priests." And as they went, they were made clean. Then one of them, when he saw that he was healed, turned back, praising God with a loud voice. He prostrated himself at Jesus' feet and thanked him. And he was a Samaritan. Then Jesus asked, "Were not ten made clean? But the other nine, where are they? Was none of them found to return and give praise to God except this foreigner?" Then he said to him, "Get up and go on your way; your faith has made you well."*
>
> LUKE 17:11–19

AS WE WORSHIP TODAY on the Sunday before Thanksgiving, let me remind you that although Thanksgiving is a uniquely American holiday, gratitude to God is universal. Thanksgiving is a national festival, but gratitude is the core of Christian worship. The Christian Church is a community that lives in gratitude. The word Eucharist means "thanksgiving." The central and most important action we do as Christians is called the Great Thanksgiving. **"When our Lord had given thanks, he broke the bread, and said, This is my body, broken for you. Do this in remembrance of me."** (1 Corinthians 11:23–24)

Certainly for the Christian, everyday is a day of gratitude to God, and in this nation the third Thursday in November has been reserved as a day of national Thanksgiving. It remembers the pilgrims who celebrated their first successful harvest at Plymouth, Massachusetts in 1621. The pilgrims were a mixed lot. Thirty-five were religious dissenters who had known persecution and exile. Sixty-six were added to the group by its financial backers. Some were listed as *saints*, that is, church members; others were listed as *strangers*, non-members. One hundred and one left England, and after sixty-six days at sea, only one had perished. However, half their number died during the first winter. They knew cold and hunger, and they knew dissension. It was dissension that brought together forty-one members of the expedition to sign the Mayflower Compact as they began life in the new world. A tiny town of twelve houses was constructed that first year, and somehow the colony survived.

By our standards they were underprivileged. Their only transportation was by foot, their clothing was inadequate, and their food came only from the sea and the forest. They had no money and no place to spend it. There were no amusements but those they created, no neighbors but Indians, and no way to communicate with their relatives back home. Yet they did have some of the greatest human assets: initiative, courage, willingness to work, hope for the future, and a boundless faith in God.

The only eyewitness description of the events that led to the first American Thanksgiving was written by Pilgrim Edward Winslow:

"Our harvest being gotten in, our governor sent four men on fowling, that we might in a special manner rejoice together after we had gathered the fruit of our labors. The four in one day killed as much fowl as, with a little help beside, served the company for almost a week. At which time, amongst other recreations, we exercised our arms, many of the Indians coming amongst us . . . whom for three days we entertained and feasted . . ."[1]

Such is the beginning of our national holiday, and yet, as early as mankind could recognize the benefits of a Higher Power, thanksgiving has been in order. For thousands of years before the pilgrims came, feasts of thanksgiving were characteristic of Native Americans, and, as I said earlier, thanksgiving forms the core of Christian worship.

In the middle of the Reformation, when the doctrines, rituals, and ecclesiastical structures of the Church were being challenged, and everything in worship seemed up for grabs, someone asked Martin Luther, "What is true worship?" The great reformer replied, "True worship is the tenth leper turning back."[2]

You remember the passage in Luke's gospel, (17:11–19) ten lepers, stopping at a distance as the Law required, crying out to Jesus: "**Master have mercy on us! . . . he said to them, 'Go and show yourselves to the priests.' And as they went they were made clean.**" But only one, a Samaritan, hated by the Jews, turned back when he saw that he was healed. He praised God with a loud voice, he fell on his face at the feet of Jesus and gave Him thanks.

Then Jesus asked, "**Were not ten made clean? Where are the other nine? Was none of them found to return and give praise to God except this foreigner?**" Then he said, "**Arise and go your way, your faith has made your whole.**"

"True worship is the tenth leper turning back." How frequently God is disappointed when we accept His blessings and never return to give Him thanks.

The Greek word here translated "made you whole" is the same word used to the sinful woman who washed His feet with her tears. Jesus said to her, "your faith *has saved you* . . . or *made you whole.*" The same word! Can it mean that ten were healed, but only one was made whole? There is no doubt that we can receive healing without gratitude, but not wholeness, not salvation. "True worship is the tenth leper turning back."

When the lepers approached Jesus, they "**stood at a distance.**" (Leviticus 13:45, 46; Numbers 5:2) Lepers lived in isolation, excluded from the human community. This remarkable moment describes a breaking down of traditional barriers. There are two barriers here: leprosy and the Samaritan's status. We know from the fourth Gospel that "Jews **have no dealings with**

Samaritans," (John 4:9) and we know from the Book of Leviticus (13:46)
that the leper was to be rigidly separated from the rest of society. Both conditions functioned as a social wall—a way to keep the undesirable separated
and "safely" isolated to prevent contamination

Lepers were outcasts, keeping their distance, crying out "Unclean! Unclean!" Samaritans were unacceptable half-breeds and religious heretics. They
too were placed outside ordinary commerce and conversation. But ever since
the tenth leper, the leprous Samaritan who turned back in gratitude and
was made whole, we have known that being an outsider is not an obstacle
to being included as a follower of Christ.

That grateful leprous Samaritan foreshadows all the Christians who were
to come after. He is the precursor of all the *Gentiles*, all the strangers, all the
destitute from all the nations who have responded to the gift of God in Jesus
Christ. As a matter of fact, by the time Luke was writing this gospel (some
sixty years after the Christ-event) these Gentiles, who had been so despised,
were turning out to be the most faithful followers of Christ. "Outsiders"
are welcome in the Kingdom of God.

We are all lepers, you and I: lepers and Samaritans. We are helpless,
alone, and touched with a terminal illness. We have absorbed the culture
and the values of the pagan world. But praise God and be filled with joy,
for when we acknowledge that healing, wholeness, and salvation are the
gifts of grace, and when we fall at the feet of God in gratitude for all He
has done, then ours is the victory, and **nothing can separate us from the
love of God in Christ Jesus our Lord."** (Romans 8:38–39) "True worship
is the tenth leper turning back."

We have so much for which to be thankful—eternal things like wholeness and salvation, but also the more transient things like "health and food
and love and friends, and everything God's goodness sends."

Rupert Brooke, the English poet, once made an inventory of the things
for which he was grateful.[3] He said, "Each item meant a memory, started
a happy thought, brought back a picture, revived a joy." So, I looked at
the simple list of "grateful-for" things, made by an English poet who died
in 1915 at the age of twenty-eight, and I discovered my own long-buried,
reawakened, grateful memories.

There was the simple listing of *"White plates and cups."* I remembered with gratitude the love and friendship that grew between Ruth's mother and me over the years. As if to solidify that friendship, she left to me a set of white-on-white Wedgewood china. I treasure that gift as a tangible reminder of her great spirit. (On special occasions, when we entertain, I sometimes let Ruth use my Wedgewood china!)

The poet was grateful for another thing: *"A strong crust of friendly bread."* When I read that, I remembered with gratitude the peace I felt during my visits to the Trappist Monastery in Conyers, Georgia. The monks offered a wonderful homemade brown bread and bean-barley coffee; they would serve it in silence but with joy, filled with the presence of God.

Brooke said he was grateful for *"Footprints in the dew"* and I recalled playing golf with an older friend early in the morning, before the dew was off the ground, leaving a trail of footprints along the fairways and across the greens. It was a special time of friendship reaching across the generations, leaving "footprints in the dew."

The poet mentioned *"The kindliness of clean sheets."* It made me think of my parents when I was a child. In the winter, on a cold night, my parents would heat the flannel sheets and tuck me into a warm bed. I felt enfolded in their love.

You must, of course, create your own inventory of thankfulness, your "memories, pictures and happy thoughts," but how difficult that must be for those who have no gratitude. For them, "Every sunset is bleached of color, every meal rendered bland and tasteless, every dream cankered, every relationship soured. Ingratitude stops prayer, represses joy, misdirects energy, and crowns the closing years with bitterness."[4] The nine lepers, all received a cleansing by God's grace, but did not turn back to praise Him, and thus they missed the fullness of His fellowship.

Some years ago, I read this by E. A. Robinson: "There are two kinds of gratitude: the sudden kind we feel for what we receive, and the larger kind we feel for what we give." It then occurred to me that the church should not have to deal with "budget." A truly Christian congregation would simply remember what God has done, count their blessings, and return His gifts in good measure, pressed down and running over. True grace, I knew, was not giving or receiving; it was not even the gift of health or wholeness; true grace was an individual sharing an intimacy with God. It's the relationship that is all-important.

While I was thinking these lofty thoughts about gratitude and generosity, the church was engaged in the annual financial campaign. It was a low-key campaign; we simply distributed lapel pins that said, "Love, Give, Share." One morning I rushed out to a breakfast meeting, and when I opened my billfold, I was embarrassed to find one of those "Love, Give, Share" buttons lodged exactly where a twenty-dollar bill used to be. Ruth had made the exchange! I had to laugh, because it was true: relationships matter most.

Those nine lepers rushing on their way never came to know how much more they needed Christ than they needed healing. I'm not sure they were any better off than before, with their cure and their ingratitude.

> Unclean! Unclean! But thou canst make me clean:
> Yet if thou clean'st me Lord, see that I be
> Like that one grateful leper of the ten
> Who ran back praising thee.
>
> But if I must forget, take back thy word:
> Be I unclean again but not ingrate.
> Before I shall forget thee, keep me, Lord,
> A sick man at thy gate.[5]

The Archbishop of Canterbury was in New Orleans in 2007, meeting with the House of Bishops of the Episcopal Church in America. His opening sermon was in response to the devastation and rebuilding he saw in New Orleans. He spoke about gratitude and what we owe to each other and to Jesus Christ. He said, "Every city and every community at some point must ask itself, 'What do we owe to one another?'" People speak about respect and the recognition of dignity, but most of all, he said, we owe each other gratitude. "The gospel tells us it is that level of owing, that level of indebtedness, that we have to introduce into our relations with one another, because the other who waits for us, especially in the stranger, in the naked, in the sick, in the imprisoned . . . the neighbor who waits for us, waits for us with a gift of life given within them. Without them we will not live."[6]

It is so startling to think that without those who need us, we will die, as Christians, as a church, as a community! That's remarkable! But it is God's way of building the communion of saints. When we share God's gift of life, we find our own life. We are all unprofitable servants, who turn back to God to find life and love and purpose. **"Whosoever will lose his life for my sake shall find it."** (Matthew16:25)

There is always a cost to caring. The nine ungrateful lepers never realized how much their healing cost the Master. In every healing miracle, in every act of compassion, someone gives something of themselves; someone is drained, weary, and spent. In Mark's Gospel (1:40), after Jesus touched a leper in a compassionate act of healing, we read: **"Jesus could no longer show himself in any town."** A leper was an outcast, unclean, and so was anyone who touched him. Compassion is costly, and it makes ingratitude all the more disappointing. When Jesus asked, "Where are the nine?" it had about it the edge of personal hurt.

Edward Spencer was a divinity student at Garrett Biblical Institute of Northwestern University in Evanston, Illinois when, on September 8, 1860, he was awakened by his fellow students saying there had been a shipwreck that night off the shore of Winnetka. An excursion ship with almost four hundred people aboard had collided with a freighter.

Ed Spencer jumped from his bed, dressed, and ran three miles to Winnetka. The lake was stormy; many would-be rescuers were discouraged by the undertow. Spencer, who was a strong swimmer, plunged in and began bringing people ashore. For six hours, he swam back and forth, battling the waves, the chilly waters, the ship's debris. He made fifteen trips and brought back fifteen people. As the light dawned, he was resting, drinking a cup of coffee, and someone shouted, "There are two more out there." In spite of his exhaustion, he plunged in again, made it to a piece of wreckage, and brought a man and a woman to safety.

In the final count, 287 people drowned; only ninety-eight survived. Seventeen were rescued by a theological student who was later carried off the beach to a hospital. Ed Spencer never became a minister; his body had been too badly weakened by the ordeal. He lived out his days an invalid in California.

Years later, as an old man, he was interviewed by a reporter in Los Angeles. One of the questions was whether he remembered anything particular about the rescue. He replied, "No, only this: of the seventeen people I saved, not one of them ever thanked me!"

All of this is simply to remind you that life is a gift, be grateful for it. "Just to get up each day is a windfall."[7] Give thanks to God! As e. e. cummings puts it in his poem:

> i thank You God for most this amazing
> day: for the leaping greenly spirits of trees
> and a blue true dream of sky; and for everything
> which is natural which is infinite which is yes
>
> (i who have died am alive again today,
> and this is the sun's birthday; this is the birth
> day of life and love and wings: and of the gay
> great happening illimitably earth)
>
> how should tasting touching hearing seeing
> breathing any–lifted from the no
> of all nothing–human merely
> being doubt unimaginable You?
>
> (now the ears of my ears awake and
> now the eyes of my eyes are opened)[8]

So, having once more been reminded of God's infinite grace, of His gift of healing and wholeness to us poor sinners, of the giving of Himself for us, the strangers, let us with praise and thanksgiving truly worship the greatness of God. Let us be "the tenth leper turning back."

In the name of Christ, *Amen.*

NOTES

1   Boorstin, Daniel J., *The Americans: The Colonial Experience*, Random House, 1958.

2   Luther, Martin.

3   Brooke, Rupert, "The Great Lover," The Collected Poems of Rupert Brooke, p. 120.

4   Newton, Joseph Fort.

5   Tynan, Katharine, "The Leper," Irish Poems, Sidgwick & Jackson Ltd, 1914.

6   Williams, Rowan, Archbishop of Canterbury, sermon preached at the Ernest N. Morial Convention Center, New Orleans LA, Sept. 21, 2007.

7   Claypool, John.

8   cummings, e. e., 1x1.

15.

The Stable and the Star

One of the great privileges of my life has been to preside over the activities of Christmas at Dauphin Way. I loved the outpouring of lavish generosity, the excited children, the glorious music, the modest yet beautiful decorations, the Candlelight Communion Service, and above all the gathering of families in wonder and in praise. For me, it was always a challenge to preach in those expectant times. I wanted the holy impulses of God to invade our practicality and our common sense and make the love that "came down at Christmas" lasting, so I preached sermons like "The Stable and the Star":

> *When they had heard the king they went their way; and lo, the star which they had seen in the East went before them, till it came to rest over the place where the child was.*
>
> MATTHEW 2:9

> *And this will be a sign for you: you will find a babe wrapped in swaddling cloths and lying in a manger.*
>
> LUKE 2:12

> There's a song in the air! There's a star in the sky!
> There's a mother's deep prayer And a baby's low cry!
> And the star rains its fire while the beautiful sing,
> For the manger of Bethlehem cradles a King![1]

AT THIS HOLY SEASON, I am always interested in how you "keep Christmas." It is fascinating to know the traditions of various families. From time to time you will hear me ask, "What are your Christmas plans? How do you and your family celebrate?"

For some, Christmas is a commercial reality. They will answer, "This is our busiest season; we do sixty percent of our business at this time of year." There are others for whom Christmas is really a family celebration. "I've been cooking for six weeks, freezing everything. They will just eat me out of house and home!" For some, Christmas stirs a latent memory of what ought to be all year long. "I've been looking for a needy family to supply with Christmas dinner and Christmas toys."

It is a remarkable season! As Shakespeare said, "So hallowed and so gracious is the time."[2] There's no way to estimate the generosity of people at Christmas. Our church, through the Society of Saint Stephen, gives toys to hundreds of children just as do other churches, the Salvation Army, the Marine Corps, and various companies and individuals. Isn't it strange that, for a short time, human hearts seem to soften and melt, and, without desiring any recognition, people search for some way to express their love and good will. One would think the average person suddenly had a vision, became star-struck, letting go for a little while the realities and necessities of life.

Now let me say that God is not fickle, nor is God seasonal. We're not zapped with a little bit of religion every December, only to have it wear off in January. That cannot be. What we see clearly illustrated at Christmas is what is always true of human nature: though we are mortal and earthly, we are created in God's image, capable of hearing God's word, following His way, seeing His star.

There is a wonderful painting in the Rijksmuseum in Amsterdam by the Dutch artist Abraham Hondius (1631–1691) called *The Annunciation to the Shepherds*. It captures that explosive moment when the angels announce the birth of Christ. The shepherds are fearful, totally captivated. They are astonished by the heavenly glory. Some are shielding their eyes from the brightness. All eyes are looking toward the heavens—all eyes but the animals'. The animals are undisturbed, as if nothing has happened; they are unaware of anything unusual. The artist is describing the nature of humankind: mortal, earthly and yet able to see the star and hear the angels' song!

It is true we live in tension between the stable and the star! Between what life requires for temporal existence and what life offers for eternal happiness. I have spent my life pointing people toward the star, and reminding them that there is more to life than bread and budgets, security and self-indulgence. But frequently, I am the one forced to say, "Don't forget, we have to pay the bills. We have to do the practical down-to-earth things."

By the same token, I am so often impressed and surprised by the business people in our church and community who make the beautifully impractical decisions to do something for God, not because it's cost-efficient, but because it is the right and lovely thing to do. That tension is always there between the *stable* and the *star*.

There are times in life when we get too much "star" and not enough "stable," when we fail to realize that necessities are realities. There are visionaries who simply feel they must burn themselves out, like a shooting star, so that the world will take notice of their cause. They are wonderful people, but we cannot all live like that.

More often, the problem is too much "stable," not enough "star." We become preoccupied with self, with our own fears and needs, and fail to follow the guiding star, trusting the Father's providence and the Father's love.

This is precisely where the Incarnation of Jesus is absolutely marvelous. Not only does it reveal the nature of God, for Christ was God, but it reveals the nature of our humanity for Christ was human. Now *there's* the paradox! How can we understand that Jesus the Christ was both God and man? We cannot comprehend, and yet we find ourselves compelled to believe. We hold fiercely to both horns of the paradox; nothing less will satisfy. The Chalcedonian Creed, written in AD 451, expresses this belief when it speaks of "our Lord Jesus Christ, perfect in Godhead and perfect in manhood, truly God and truly man . . . in two natures, inconfusedly, immutably, indivisibly, inseparably . . . in one person . . ."

In the early years of the Church there were those who believed that Jesus was all divine without any humanity. They believed that He did not suffer, He did not hunger, and He did not feel the pathos of man or the pain of the Cross. He could not feel, for He was *only spirit*. The Church could not accept that. Still others believed that Jesus was not God at all, but *fully human*. He was simply the logical apex of humanity reaching up for God. And neither could the Church accept that.

So orthodox Christianity holds on to the paradox that Jesus the Christ is fully God and fully man, knowing that we cannot understand it, but neither can we let it go. In that divine Incarnation, where "He became as we are that we might become as He is,"[3] there is displayed the tension between the vision and the practicality, between this world and the world beyond. It is a tension played out in the common experience of our "everyday."

Take as an illustration the remarkable changes that occurred in Russia and the former Soviet bloc. Deny the aspirations and the vision of people long enough, and they are willing to pay any price, even their own lives, for change. People must be allowed to follow their ambitions and their dreams, otherwise there is too much stable and not enough star.

However, when, in 1989, the leaders of East and West Germany met at the Brandenburg Gate and released doves of peace, or when military and political leaders apologize to the people for the mistreatment they have imposed, or dictators are deposed, if you think there are no remaining problems such as economic viability and the establishment of democratic procedures and the responsibilities of liberty, if you think all the problems are over when the doves have been released, then you've got too much star and not enough stable.

Let me talk with you a moment about the Church, for we are the Church, you and I. Some are more involved in its program than others, but most of us are here because we are believers, and believers constitute the Church. What we need at this moment is for the Church to be able to see the star.

Certainly I do not minimize the practical realities. This church has not denied or ignored the physical needs of people. We have attempted to minister to the whole person. We have condemned injustice. We have fed the poor. We have operated the church on a business-like basis. We recognize the social realities of evangelism. We try to be as practical as we can. (As a matter of fact, if some of our ladies had been present at the birth of Jesus, they would have put fresh hay in the manger, rocked the baby, and collected food and blankets for the family. They would have found them better quarters and arranged for a caravan to take them home—all necessary things.) But, my soul, I hope we would not miss the star and the meaning of God's great gift!

So this Christmas, while there is yet time, I urge you to look for the star. Shake yourself free from the "stable syndrome." At this moment we need to *see the star.* There is the danger of becoming stuck in the familiar. When we don't expect anything unusual to happen, we fail to realize that the Christian faith, taken seriously, will truly change our lives.

W. H. Auden, describing the shepherds hearing the angel voices has the shepherds say:

> Tonight for the first time
> the prison gates have opened,
> Music and sudden light
> Have interrupted our routine tonight—
> And swept the filth of habit from our hearts—
> O here and now the endless journey starts.[4]

We need to see the star and hear the angels sing.

It is to the great credit of children that they can become "lost in wonder, love, and praise," and they can believe in miracles. A miracle has been defined as putting the event before the explanation. We grown ups must explain everything; analyze everything, before we can believe it. It is true as Socrates said, "The unexamined life is not worth living," but it is also true that the un-lived life is not worth examining! We need to know the wonder and joy and magnificence of *Emmanuel,* "God with us!"

Therefore, what I exhort you to do about Christmas is to "keep it"—to hold on to the glory and the wonder of Christmas all year long.

> Whatever else be lost among the years
> Let us keep Christmas still a shining thing:
> Let us hold close one day, remembering
> Its poignant meaning for the hearts of men.
> Let us get back our child-like faith again.[5]

This year, while there's still time, let's try reflecting, remembering, getting back our "child-like faith."

The return of that child-like faith, that feeling of being "star-struck," is relatively easy in families to whom a child is born at Christmas. The waiting, the expectations, the hopes and dreams showered on a new life, the miracle of it all, causes the birth of Christ to become more real to them. This new expression of their own love helps them to behold the love of God. These families make all the practical arrangements, of course, but somehow it is easier to see the star.

It is also not uncommon for the light of God to shine in the midst of some tragedy at Christmas—the loss of a loved one, a natural disaster, the calamity of war. I see it in the homeless here at home and the refugees abroad. Somehow knowing that Mary and Joseph experienced the same forlornness of having no place in the world helps them to depend on that divine love which alone can save. In adversity, there are always people of faith who gain a certain peace, an awareness of God's presence, and in the midst of stable life they see the star.

I have watched it on every Christmas Eve—that same feeling of wonder calmly falling over those who arrive at church for the Christmas Eve Communion. People en route to, or coming from, a Christmas dinner, some who still have last-minute preparations before Christmas morning . . . so much to do. But for a moment, they step inside the quiet, candle-lit beauty of the church. Families who love each other sit for a little while in silence, conscious of the presence of God who loves them most of all, and those who are far seem near and the near becomes far. They reflect for a moment on their blessings, and on the coming of Christ with His costly sacrifice, and they commune. They are with God. Then, surrounded by the Father's steadfast love, these star-struck people go out into the night, into the future, confident to be guided by the star of Bethlehem!

In the name of Christ, *Amen.*

NOTES

1   Holland, Josiah G., 1874.

2   Shakespeare, William, *Hamlet*, Act I.

3   St. Athanasius, 4th C., *The Incarnation of the Word*.

4   Auden, W. H., "For the Time Being, a Christmas Oratorio."

5   Crowell, Grace Noll, "Whatever Be Lost Among the Year."

16.

A Song of Ascent

One Sunday after church a perceptive layman said to me, "It is a joy to see how easily all of you communicate and work together during worship." I was surprised, not realizing that anyone would notice. That casual remark reminded me how much I loved the majestic worship at Dauphin Way—the grand organ, the choral music, the carefully planned liturgy, the ministry to children, the hymns and the scripture and the sermon all woven into one seamless shout of praise. I doubt if my gratitude was ever expressed adequately to the associate ministers, the ministers of music, the choir, and all who freely gave their insight and inspiration to the careful planning and conduct of worship. Advancing up the steps of the church, climbing the seven steps to the pulpit, hopefully ascending the stairway to heaven, I was aware that Dauphin Way always provided for me a more than adequate framework for the worship of God. One Palm Sunday, amid the shouts of "Hallelujah," and hoping that others would be touched as well by the mystery and the majesty of worship, I preached "A Song of Ascent":

With that Jesus went forward and began the ascent to Jerusalem. As he approached Bethphage and Bethany at the hill called Olivet, he sent two of the disciples with these instructions: "Go to the village opposite; as you enter it you will find tethered there a colt which no one has yet ridden. Untie it and bring it here. If anyone asks why you are untying it, say, 'Our Master needs it.'" The two went on their errand and found it as he had told them; and while they were untying the colt, its owners asked, "Why are you untying that colt?" They answered, "Our Master needs it." So they brought the colt to Jesus. Then they threw their cloaks on the colt, for Jesus to mount, and they carpeted the road with them as he went on his way. And now, as he approached the descent from the Mount of Olives, the whole company of his disciples in their joy began to sing aloud the praises of God for all the great things they had seen:

"Blessings on him who comes as king in the name of the Lord! Peace in heaven, glory in highest heaven!"

Some Pharisees who were in the crowd said to him, "Master, reprimand your disciples." He answered, "I tell you, if my disciples keep silence the stones will shout aloud."

LUKE 19:28–40 (NEB)

TODAY'S SCRIPTURE BEGINS IN this way: "Jesus went forward and began the ascent to Jerusalem." The ascent to Jerusalem from Jericho was an incline of some twenty miles up a road that rose nearly four thousand feet to the crest of the Mount of Olives. Jerusalem is situated on the summit of the Judean mountains. It was a glorious ascent, but to the devout Jews it was more than geography. To climb Mount Zion was an aspiration, an aspiration felt in the mind, heart and spirit of a people reaching upward toward the Holy City of God.

There are fifteen psalms in the Psalter, 120–134, marked in the early manuscripts as "A Song of Ascents." They were so labeled because these were the songs the people sang as they ascended to Jerusalem on a pilgrimage to worship during one of the great festivals. In later years, according to the Mishnah, the Levites would sing these fifteen psalms on the fifteen Temple steps leading from the Court of the Women to the Court of the Israelites. These psalms provide a classic collection of triumphant praise. You know many of them; they are among your favorites:

> I will lift up mine eyes unto the hills –
> From whence cometh my help? (121:1)

> Unless the Lord builds the house,
> They labor in vain who build it. (127:1)

Out of the depths I have cried unto you, O Lord;
Lord, hear my voice! (130:1)

Behold, how good and how pleasant it is
For brethren to dwell together in unity. (133:1)

I was glad when they said unto me,
Let us go into the house of the Lord. (122:1)

It is therefore easy to understand that when the Rabbi from Nazareth began to ascend the upward road from Jericho to Jerusalem, the disciples broke out in song. In great joy, they sang the praises of God: "**Blessed is the king who comes in the name of the Lord. Peace in heaven and glory in the highest.**" (Luke 19:38) It sounded like the song the angels sang when Christ the King was born, and I for one hope the Christian Church never loses its triumphant song of praise!

In the Old Testament book of Numbers, there is a remarkable story of how the King of Moab tried to destroy the people of Israel by hiring a prophet to curse them. The Israelite army was encamped in tents, clustered together on the plain, quite unconscious of the dark conspiracy that was brewing on the heights above. There in the mountain, Balak, the Moabite king, badgered his hireling prophet, Balaam. He hurried him from one point to another, urging him to use his black arts of magic and wizardry to bring a spell or a blight upon Israel camped in the plain below.

Balaam looked down at the tents of Israel, and said to the king, "You may have paid me well, you may be the monarch of Moab, but I cannot do it. I cannot curse what God has blessed."

But the king persisted, "You must and you shall. Try again! Come to another vantage point where you can see only a part of the army of Israel, and you can try from there." And so he harassed, the luckless prophet, but always the evil plan was thwarted, and always came the same infuriating answer: "I cannot do it. King or no king, bribe or no bribe, I cannot curse what God has blessed."[1] Then the prophet said, "I tell you Balak, Prince of Moab, there is no spell, no magic in the world that will bind or shackle that host of Israel for "**the Lord their God is with them, and the shout of a King is among them.**" (Numbers 23:21)

What a marvelous word! It anticipates Palm Sunday: the Lord their God was with them and the people shouted that he was their King. "**Blessed is the King who comes in the name of the Lord! Peace in heaven and glory in the highest!**"

How earnestly we trust that it will always be true of the New Israel, the Church of Jesus Christ, that "**the Lord their God is with them and the shout of a King is among them.**" No evil can defeat us when we are in the presence of God and proclaim His Son as the King of Kings. And what a gracious King He is:

> His scepter is his kindliness,
> His grandeur is his grace,
> His royalty is holiness,
> And love is in his face.[2]

Historically, what created the Israel of the desert and the Promised Land—what constituted them as a community, an army, and eventually a nation—was not their legal system, their organization, or their leadership. What created the Promised Land of Israel was this one thing which the prophet Balaam had stumbled upon unwittingly: "**The Lord their God was with them and the shout of a King was among them.**"

It is equally true for the New Israel, the Christian Church. It does not exist because of its orthodoxy, its apostolic succession, or its influential patronage. The true Church exists here on earth because of the vitality of God's Spirit: "**The Lord our God is with us and the shout of a king is among us.**"

That "shout of the King" has been heard through the centuries in major movements, whenever a Francis, a Luther, a Wesley has given the Church back its soul, and in a million smaller victories where Christians have found the faith to march with a ringing, joyful confidence, a song of ascent, the shout of the King: "**Blessed is the king who comes in the name of the Lord.**"

Think of that quiet confidence and unshakable joy that would be yours, just by being in the presence of Christ. One morning, before going into to preach, Leslie Weatherhead imagined how it might be if Jesus were present. He wrote, "In imagination I am in the synagogue, too, waiting for the service to begin. I am spiritually hungry, longing for some message from God, some assurance that man is not left alone. Then Jesus enters. I see His quiet, yet radiant, face. I note the serenity of His whole bearing. He kneels and then sits, relaxed and happy to be with God's people on God's day. I find myself wishing He were nearer to me. Yet His entry has made a difference to us all. The whole spiritual temperature has risen. A strange sense of quiet joy and well-being seems to seep into my heart. I become sure of God and sure that I am forgiven, loved, understood, accepted."

That day, before worship, Dr. Weatherhead wrote this prayer. O Lord may "Thy spirit emanate from me, and today, in the worship of the sanctuary, may I make it easier for others to pray, easier for others to believe in God and to find Him, easier for troubled minds to find peace and the heavy-laden rest."[3]

I know there are those who say this "Song of Ascent" is sheer exuberance, unbridled emotionalism. They say we Christians ought to hear the Cry of Dereliction rather than "the shout of a King." They say we are servants not celebrants. There is truth in that. It is only right that the Church should agonize over the Third World, the miseries of nations victimized by war, people enslaved by famine, poverty, and discrimination. We cannot rest our efforts to remedy injustice; there is no argument with that. It is right that with all our strength we should be serving the suffering, the downtrodden, the oppressed, and doing so in the name of Christ.

We do just that when we deliver Meals-On-Wheels, provide for the indigent, tutor in the inner city, visit the jails, or give wheelchairs to Costa Rica and relief to Haiti. All next week, observing the Passion of our Lord we will hear the Cry of Dereliction. We will agonize over the suffering world; it is mete and right for the Christian so to do. Indeed, I make no apology for the seriousness of the Christian faith. We cannot take it casually. There is a required discipline that is implicit in the Christian experience.

It would be the greatest mistake to neglect "the deep things of God," to treat all life lightly, as if this life were some sort of "fool's paradise." It is as Harry Emerson Fosdick said, "Gay moods can be answered by many gaieties; aesthetic moods can be answered by many kinds of beauty; affectionate moods can be answered by many forms of human love. But there is a real tragedy for those who have no religious faith . . . Someday life will take them into the depths, and the deep in them will call out for some great deep to answer it. What then, if there is no deep there?"[4]

All that is true! We will see that reality unvarnished when Holy Week plunges us again into the tomb of Jesus and hangs us on His Cross, but it is also true that Christians have not witnessed enough about their joy. Jesus was **"a man of sorrows and acquainted with grief,"** (Isaiah 53:3) but that was only half the portrait. The Man from Nazareth was filled with joy. He said: **"These things have I spoken to you, that my joy may be in you, and that your joy may be full."** (John 15:11)

That sacred joy is all through the Bible: **"Blessed are ye that weep now, for ye shall laugh."** Remember how the Psalmist says **"He who sits in the heavens, laughs."** (2:4) What a wonderful description of God! It describes His joy beyond all earthly loss or pain.

When Dante wrote *The Divine Comedy*, which, by the way, he simply named, "Comedy," he did so in order to show the triumph of God's love throughout the created universe. In this allegorical poem, Dante is guided through Hell until he finally climbs his way to Paradise. When he arrives in Paradise, he hears a chorus of angels, which he says "seemed like the laughter of the universe." How true! There is no laughter in Hell, for Hell is a place where hope does not exist. Laughter is the voice of *faith*!

There is such a great joy in the good news that those who receive it cannot keep it to themselves. The apostles were so excited at Pentecost that onlookers thought they were drunk. The early Franciscans were so delighted with their new knowledge of God, they had to be reproved for laughing in church. That joyous praise and celebration flows throughout the Bible. When Jerusalem was in ruins Isaiah said: **"Sing together, ye waste places of Jerusalem, for the Lord has comforted his people and has redeemed Jerusalem."** (Isaiah 52:9)

Robert Burns was quite correct:

If happiness hath not her seat
And center in the breast,
We may be wise, or rich, or great,
But never can be blest.[5]

One of the great lessons of joyful Christianity is not to take oneself too seriously. This life, of course, is tremendously important, but it is not ultimately important. Humor teaches us humility and, by contrast, shows us how far all human beings fall short of the glory of God. To laugh at ourselves reminds us of our awkwardness in this life and our hope for perfection in the life to come.

We have always known the ill effects of fear, dread, depression, and hate on the human organism. Now we are beginning to realize the positive effects of laughter. Dr. John Stehlin is an oncologist at St. Joseph Hospital in Houston. He works with patients whose prospects for recovery are considered to be slight. He emphasizes their will to live and their confidence in the treatment. The cancer floor is a place of good humor and optimism; it is called "The Living Room." As the proverb says, **"A merry heart doeth good like a medicine."** (Proverbs 17:22)

We cannot surrender the shout of praise that God is King and reigns victorious. It is just not right for Christians to worship without a song of gladness. Indeed, how can we worship at all without a vivid sense of the transcendent, without opening the windows to an unseen reality, without some beam of supernatural light streaming in from the celestial city. Christians cannot thrive or survive without the presence of God and the shout of a King.

Do you remember the parables of Jesus about the unfinished tower and the king's rash warfare? No one builds a tower without first counting the cost, and no king with ten thousand soldiers declares war on another with twenty thousand soldiers. These parables are not the Lord's way of discouraging our impulsive enlistment in the Christian cause; they illustrate the Christian confidence in God. You wouldn't start a war you couldn't win or build a tower you couldn't finish. Neither would God. His kingdom can be resisted, but it cannot be overcome. God has no unfinished towers, no wars He will not win. He has the means to win the war against evil, and He means to win!

For that reason we must not be discouraged; God's way will win. It is better to forgive than to avenge, better to be prayerful than anxious, better to be humble than proud, better to reconcile than to divide, better to love than to hate. Now some say that won't work in a world like this. It will! God is not going to start a war He can't win. Trust Him, believe Him, try Him. He will surprise you with His miracles of love.

I'll tell you something else about this Christian life. When you are ascending toward Jerusalem with a song in you heart and praise for your King, you attain a different view, a new perspective. Jesus said, **"My kingdom is not of this world."** I'm sure, if He had wished, Jesus could have ruled the world. But He would not have it so. This world was not His kingdom.

Yet certainly, He is a King! So, over what kind of kingdom does He wish to reign? He wishes to reign over a kingdom of kings! No monarch cares to rule over a kingdom of savages or animals. The Kingdom of Christ is a kingdom of love where no one seeks to be above another, and every person is both a servant and a sovereign.

One more thing that is so fundamental: we reach for fellowship with the living God. That is the great human ascent; our worship is both friendship with Christ and adoration of God, His Father. It is so amazing that earthly human beings might aspire to such glorious heights! The Psalmist spoke for all of us: **"My heart and my flesh cry out for the living God."** (84:2) We reach out to God in many ways: by prayer and Christian study, in association with Christian people, through generosity and charity. Above all, we ascend into the presence of God through worship. It is here that finding Him we find ourselves, and here we align ourselves with the purposes and ministry of the Almighty. In worship we create something eternal, we redeem something of value. All our living becomes focused on praising God, and in so doing we discover a deep and abiding joy!

> O the sheer joy of it!
> Working with God,
> Running his errands,

Waiting his nod,
Building his heaven
On common sod.
O the sheer joy of it!
Working with God.[6]

Max Lucado describes the wonder of this discovery, the wonder of discovering that joyful bond between us and our heavenly Father. He says, "If you were the only person on earth, the earth would look exactly the same. The Himalayas would still have their drama and the Caribbean would still have its charm . . . If you were the sole pilgrim on this globe, God would not diminish its beauty one degree . . . He did it all for you."[7]

O my soul, what joy to think He loves me so! How personal are the words of the prophet Zephaniah: "**The Lord your God is with you; the mighty One will save you. He will rejoice over you. You will rest in his love; he will sing and be joyful about you.**" (3:17)

God's great love for us is so amazing—no wonder we Christians celebrate! And this is what we celebrate: that now we know the great love of God through Jesus Christ His Son. "**The Lord our God is with us, and the shout of the King is among us.**"

In the name of Christ, *Amen.*

Notes

1   Stewart, James S., *King For Ever*, Abingdon Press, p. 9.
2   Pennewell, Almer T., "So Lowly Doth the Savior Ride," 1966.
3   Weatherhead, Leslie.
4   Fosdick, Harry Emerson.
5   Burns, Robert, "Epistle to Davie, a Brother Poet," 1785.
6   Cushman, Ralph Spaulding, "O the Sheer Joy of It."
7   Lucado, Max, *One Incredible Moment*, J. Countryman, 2006, p. 67.

17.

The Weight of a Petal

Whedn I retired the first time, in 1990, Ruth and I moved into a recreational home we had built on Fowl River in south Mobile County. Retirement was made more pleasant because our home is near the beautiful and historic Bellingrath Gardens and Home. As we are able, we walk the gardens, attend the workshops, eat at the restaurant, browse through the gift shop. We have been enriched by the friendship of many of the garden staff, especially the director and his wife, Dr. and Mrs. William E. Barrick. The founders of the Gardens, Mr. and Mrs. Walter Bellingrath, were devoted Christians, and being mindful of that heritage, Dr. Barrick has offered the community an Easter Sunrise Service in that beautiful garden. The floral location reminded me of the resurrection in "Joseph's Lovely Garden." At Bellingrath Gardens, early on Easter Morning, 2009, I preached "The Weight of a Petal":

> As they were saying this, Jesus himself stood among them. But they were startled and frightened, and supposed that they saw a spirit. And he said to them, "Why are you troubled, and why do questionings rise in your hearts? See my hands and my feet, that it is I myself; handle me, and see; for a spirit has not flesh and bones as you see that I have." And while they still disbelieved for joy, and wondered, he said to them, "Have you anything here to eat?" They gave him a piece of broiled fish, and he took it and ate before them. Then he said to them, "These are my words which I spoke to you, while I was still with you, that everything written about me in the law of Moses and the prophets and the psalms must be fulfilled." Then he opened their minds to understand the scriptures, and said to them, "Thus it is written, that the Christ

should suffer and on the third day rise from the dead, and that repentance and forgiveness of sins should be preached in his name to all nations, beginning from Jerusalem. You are witnesses of these things."

LUKE 24:36–48

RUTH AND I HAVE long loved Bellingrath Gardens. We visited the gardens frequently in the first years of our marriage. The gardens then were but twenty years old, and Mr. Bellingrath was still alive. It has always been a special place for us.

George Bernard Shaw said, "The best place to seek God is in a garden. You can dig for him there."[1] So, digging for God in the gardens, thinking of the rich Christian heritage of Walter and Bessie Bellingrath, considering the wonder of Easter and the beauty of spring, I decided to talk about the amazing providence of God, the weight of a petal.

The hungering for new birth is universal. Before the Christian era, the Teutons of northern Europe, and the Angles and the Saxons, honored *Eostre*, the goddess of new life. The greatest miracle they knew was spring breaking the death-hold of winter. But now we know that the same God who gave the earth a new birth of spring has also given humankind the promise of new life in Christ. Christina Rossetti describes that fundamental connection:

> Spring bursts today,
> For Christ is risen and all the earth's at play.
> Break forth this morn
> In roses, thou but yesterday a thorn.
> Uplift thy head,
> O pure white lily through the winter dead.
> Sing, creatures, sing,
> Angels and men and birds and everything.[2]

That bright floral context is not as foreign to the Bible as you might think. When the Song of Solomon says, "**I am a rose of Sharon, a lily of the valley,**" what Christian does not apply it to his Lord? Or, who among us can forget the gospel hymn, "He's the lily of the valley, the bright and morning star."[3]

Loren Eiseley, anthropologist and naturalist, has a book called *The Immense Journey* which is both science and literature. He describes the sudden development of flowering plants, which actually provided the energy for warm-blooded mammals. The agile brain of warm-blooded creatures demands a high consumption of oxygen and food in concentrated forms. Flowering plants provided that energy and changed the nature of the living world. Eiseley said, "Somewhere, just a short time before the close of the Age of Reptiles, there occurred a soundless, violent explosion. It marked the emergence of the angiosperms—the seedpods of the flowering plants. Even the evolutionist, Charles Darwin, called them 'an abominable mystery,' because they appeared so suddenly and spread so fast. Agriculture is almost entirely dependent on angiosperms. So it is fair to say flowers changed the face of the planet . . .

"Today we know that the appearance of the flowers paralleled the equally mystifying emergence of man . . . even human life was made possible by this new store of energy in concentrated form." Eiseley said: "The weight of a petal has changed the face of the world and made it ours."[4]

That quiet miracle, that petal-weight that tipped the scale and changed the world, is like the miracle that raised Christ from the dead. Quiet and powerful, diverse and filled with endless ramifications, beautiful and mysterious, that single Resurrection of Christ was the weight of a petal that changed the world.

You must remember that at first, the Resurrection was not widely celebrated. It was not a community festival. The risen Christ appeared to His friends, to His disciples, and once appeared to more than five hundred followers. They viewed the miraculous appearance with fear and trembling. At first, they only dared to wonder; they whispered about what they had seen and heard. They spoke quietly, mysteriously, and excitedly. To say the very least, it was not expected, nor was it understood.

For example, when the Sabbath was over, three of the women brought aromatic oils to the tomb in order to anoint the body. They were dumbfounded to find no crucified remains but instead a young man in a white robe, who said, "**He is risen!**" The women fled the tomb, according to the scripture, "**for fear and astonishment had come upon them, and they said nothing to anyone, for they were afraid.**" (Mark 16:8)

The great truth came quietly at first, deeply hidden within the soul, like a seed in the fertile ground—then, gradually blossoming, like fruit trees in an orchard, until the glory could not be hidden or ignored. The weight of a petal had changed the world.

Oh, believe the Resurrection earnestly! It is central to our faith! It is life to the spirit! The risen Christ is no less transforming to the soul of man than spring to barren winter. Resurrection and spring are both the heralds of new life.

On the surface, it may appear that nothing has changed. Christians still work and play, save and dream, love and hope like everyone else. But everything has changed! Now we see life differently. We live with confidence after the Christ-event, for we are now certain of the Father's love. Resurrection is our assurance of the providence of God. There we see, as in the twinkling of an eye, that God has prepared for our every need.

Do you remember the classic little book by William E. Barrett, *The Lilies of the Field?*" In the movie adaptation, Sidney Poitier played the part of Homer Smith. It is the strangely beautiful story of a black Baptist drifter who builds a church for a group of German Catholic nuns in the southwest U. S. First, Homer Smith offers to work if they will pay him. Mother Maria believes that God has sent him to help, so why should they pay him. Their traditions are different, but they both know the Bible. Their languages are different, so he writes the reference, Luke 10:7: "**The laborer is worthy of his hire.**" She writes Proverbs 1:14: "**Cast thy lot among us; let us all have one purse.**" He shakes his head and says, "No, I am poor; I work for wages." She understands him; she writes Matthew 6:28: "**Why take ye thought for raiment? Consider the lilies of the field . . .**"

Oh, it is such a penetrating question for our chaotic world! Should we not "**consider the lilies of the field, how they grow; they toil not neither do they spin: and yet I say unto you that even Solomon in all his glory was not arrayed like one of these . . . O, ye of little faith.**" (Matthew 6:28–29,30)

Yes, consider the providence of God, His foresight and preparation.

Consider the lilies, how they grow, how anything grows, how a seed gets to be a flower, how a blob of protoplasm gets to be a child, then a man, a mind mature? How? "What pushes it to grow? What gives the cell the urge and intelligence to divide and multiply itself?" We might risk an explanation from the near side, the scientific side, the observable side, but what is on the other side? "Underlying every utterance of Jesus is the conviction that everything that lives is planted deeply in the providence of God, is enveloped by it, enfolded by it, dependent on it and apart from it nothing can exist."[5]

The amazing providence of God! Think of the wide cooperation of powerful, invisible, planetary forces that are required to make a tiny flower or a blade of grass. The sun a hundred million miles away shines down, the earth turns, the seasons follow in their order, the tides move. Warm air rises from the oceans, the lightning flash releases nourishing nitrogen and the rainstorm brings it to the earth.[6] All for a tiny seed. So Francis Thompson said one cannot pluck a flower without troubling a star:

> There's part of the sun in an apple,
> And part of the moon in a rose,
> And part of the flaming Pleiades
> In every leaf that grows.[7]

In the same way, God's mysterious power brings forth the risen Christ, assuring Christians that **"Because I live, you shall live also!"** Following that bright morning in Joseph's lovely garden, we have been astonished to behold life in the place of death, goodness in the place of evil, victory overcoming defeat. The weight of a petal has changed the world.

To those without faith, the Christian perspective must seem to be a topsy-turvy way of looking at the world. Saint Paul traveled to Thessalonica where he preached in the synagogue for three weeks and argued from the scriptures, saying, **"This Jesus is the Christ."** Finally, Jason and some of the other new believers were dragged before the city magistrates, and accusers said, **"Jason has received these men who have turned the world upside down."** (Acts 17:6–7)

Yes indeed, the risen Christ turned the world upside down! It is not the same any more. G. K. Chesterton has a wonderful biography of Saint Francis of Assisi. He describes that profound spiritual revolution that transformed a fashionable playboy into a saint. Francis was cavalier, boastful, in search of prominence, but unexpectedly, he began to change. He was overcome with generosity; he was overwhelmed by the presence of God. The impact was so tremendous that he retreated into a cave alone, spending long hours in searching prayer. Chesterton said when Francis came out of that cave, "He looked at the world as differently from other men as if he had come out of the dark hole walking on his hands."[8]

There is such penetrating truth in that description. It is an explanation of inversion; it is the way Christians, after the Resurrection, observe the world. If a person looks at the world upside down, reversed, with all the towers and the trees hanging down, the effect would be to emphasize the idea of dependence. Actually the word dependence literally means "hanging down." It is a way of looking at the whole world as if it were dependent on God. As Job said, God **"hangs the world on nothing."** (26:7) That imagery of the saint walking on his hands is a beautiful description of the spiritual transformation that took place in the life of Saint Francis. Now transformed, he would see his beloved city upside down. Not a single detail would be changed, except that the massive foundations of the city, which before portrayed safety and permanence, would now be in peril. He would be thankful to God that it had not fallen, that the whole cosmos had not dropped and shattered like crashing crystal. As Chesterton said, "Perhaps Saint Peter saw the world so, when he was crucified head-downwards."[9] The whole universe is dependent on the providence of God!

If you look at the principalities and powers of this world from that perspective, even a powerful nation like our own is fragile and vulnerable. All these visible, tangible forms are transient; they will pass away. Only the invisible things—faith, hope, love—are permanent.

The truth is that we ourselves are mortal; there is no ultimate security in this life. Try as we may to deny death, behind our insecurity, behind the dread of uselessness, behind the easy approach of depression, is the specter of death. It is what William James called "the worm at the core of man's pretensions to happiness."[10] We are mortal. The same leaky boat in these wild waters bears us all.

The biblical message does not gloss over the prospect of death, even the death of Jesus. Matthew and John say, "**he gave up his spirit . . .**" Mark and Luke, he "**breathed his last.**" The demise of Jesus is described in clear detail: the nails, the cross, the torment by His captors, the release of His spirit, the grief of His friends, the thrust of the spear. Not only His death, but His burial is recited ever so carefully: the body was wrapped and laid in a tomb, the stone was rolled against the door. The Prince of glory died.

The Roman world took little notice of the crucifixion of Jesus because death is universal. The Resurrection of Jesus was also unnoticed outside that circle of friends who followed Him, because new life in Christ was yet unknown. Nevertheless, gradually, increasingly, the world has come to know that whenever a person is confronted by the Christ-event, the life, death, and Resurrection of Jesus, there is an assurance of life beyond death, of salvation beyond sin, and of joy beyond suffering. "**He who raised Christ Jesus from the dead, will give life to your mortal bodies also.**" (Romans 8:11)

My dear friends, I confess I am often concerned about the future; I become anxious about tomorrow. Will there be war or peace? Will the present war be contained or will it fuel a wider conflagration? Is there any peaceful solution between Israel and the Palestinians, between the West and radical Islam? Will our national life accommodate diversity within community? Will there be economic prosperity or recession? Will our culture continue to be corrupted by moral decline? Will technology praise God or plunder Him? Will faith in Christ grow and flower, or will it become a neglected garden while others flourish? And as for me and mine, or you and yours, what will be our heritage?

Oh, ye of little faith! After hearing these concerns, can you not also hear the Lord saying, "**Fear not, little flock, for it is your Father's good pleasure to give you the kingdom.**" Luke 12:32)

Our journey here will always be "in harm's way." Our decisions will be difficult, our route treacherous. "Through many dangers, toils and snares, I have already come." And yet, I am certain that God's grace, His saving providence, will lead us safely home.

So it is no wonder people of the Resurrection Faith sing "Hallelujah" on Easter morn! Christians cannot help but sing! There is no other appropriate response to the Resurrection. In the midst of a turbulent second century, Pliny reported to the Roman emperor that the most remarkable thing about the "new sect" of Christians is that they keep singing in their meeting places. Saint Chrysostom said, "All come together with us to sing, and in it they unitedly join, the young and old, the rich and the poor, women and men, slaves and free, all send forth one melody."

So, let Christians sing.

> Sing with all the saints in glory,
>
> Sing the resurrection song.
>
> Death and sorrow, earth's dark story
>
> To the former days belong.
>
> Life eternal! Heaven rejoices;
>
> Jesus lives, who once was dead,
>
> Join we now the deathless voices;
>
> Child of God lift up your head![11]

In the name of Christ, *Amen.*

Notes

1 Shaw, George Bernard, *The Adventures of the Black Girl in Her Search for God*, Constable & Co., 1932.

2 Rossetti, Christina, "An Easter Carol," 1894.

3 Frye, William C., 1881.

4 Eiseley, Loren, *The Immense Journey*, Random House, 1946, p. 77.

5 Hamilton, Wallace, *Serendipity*, Fleming H. Revell Co., 1965, p. 39,40.

6 Ibid, p. 41.

7 Bamberger, Augustus Wright, "Out of the Vast."

8 Chesterton, C. K., *St. Francis of Assisi*, Doubleday, 1937, p. 63.

9 Ibid, p. 67.

10 James, William, "The Varieties of Religious Experience," Gifford Lectures, University of Edinburgh, 1902.

11 Irons, William J., 1873.

18.

He is Risen, Indeed!

Many years ago, my associate, Dr. Tim Thompson, preached at Dauphin Way on the Sunday after Easter. He began by saying, "Every associate pastor in America is preaching today!" Dr. Thompson is now pastor of Frazer United Methodist Church in Montgomery, Alabama, one of Methodism's greatest churches. He now knows from firsthand experience that it is one of the greatest pleasures and one of the greatest responsibilities of a senior minister to preach to a full house in a great church on Easter Sunday. After being retired for almost twenty years I never thought I would know that joy again. Yet, much to my surprise, on Easter Sunday, April 4, 2010, I found myself the Interim Senior Pastor at Dauphin Way. It seemed almost to apply to me personally when I chose the Easter sermon title, "He is Risen, Indeed!":

> *That very day two of them were going to a village named Emmaus, about seven miles from Jerusalem, and talking with each other about all these things that had happened. While they were talking and discussing together, Jesus himself drew near and went with them. But their eyes were kept from recognizing him. And he said to them, "What is this conversation which you are holding with each other as you walk?" And they stood still, looking sad. Then one of them, named Cleopas, answered him, "Are you the only visitor to Jerusalem who does not know the things that have happened there in these days?" And he said to them, "What things?" And they said to him, "Concerning Jesus of Nazareth, who was a prophet mighty in deed and word before God and all the people, and how our chief priests and rulers delivered him up to be condemned to death, and crucified him.*

But we had hoped that he was the one to redeem Israel . . ."
So they drew near to the village to which they were going. He
appeared to be going further, but they constrained him, saying,
"Stay with us, for it is toward evening and the day is now far
spent." So he went in to stay with them. When he was at table
with them, he took the bread and blessed, and broke it, and gave
it to them. And he vanished out of their sight.
They said to each other, "Did not our hearts burn within us while
he talked to us on the road, while he opened to us the scriptures?"
And they rose that same hour and returned to Jerusalem; and
they found the eleven gathered together and those who were with
them, who said, "The Lord has risen indeed, and has appeared to
Simon!"

LUKE 24:13–21, 28–34

I CONFESS TO YOU that I love Easter! I love the miracle of spring. I love the beauty of the Church on Easter morning. I love the celebration and the crowds. I love the victory of the Resurrection and I delight in the fact that the central theme of the chancel window in our church is the Resurrection. It cannot be said too emphatically that the Resurrection must be taken seriously; *it is the central tenet of the Christian faith.* **"If Christ has not been raised then our preaching is in vain, and your believing it is in vain."** (I Cor. 15:14)

The Biblical account, our faith history, and the results of historical research tell us a great deal about the consequences of the Resurrection, but what actually happened is shrouded in mystery. What was it, a molecular transformation, a physical-to-spiritual energy exchange? Was it permanence given to moral qualities? In truth, we don't know.

Frederick Buechner said it so well: "I can tell you this: that what I believed happened, and what in faith and great joy I proclaim to you is that he somehow got up, with the life in him again, and the glory upon him. And I speak very plainly here, very unfancifully, even though I don't understand well my own language. I was not there to see it anymore than I was awake to see the sunrise this morning, but I affirm it as surely as I do that by God's grace the sun did rise this morning, because that is why the world is flooded with light. That is all we know, all we need to know that somehow he got up with the life in him and glory upon him and the world is flooded with light."[1]

A few years ago the cover story of *U.S. News and World Report* was called "The Last Days of Jesus." It said that now theologians were shedding new light on the last days of Jesus. I really didn't find any new information, but the closing paragraph was absolutely correct regarding the Resurrection: "Yet even the most skeptical biblical scholars concede that something extraordinary happened in Jerusalem after Good Friday to account for the radical change in the behavior of the disciples. Within a few weeks they were boldly preaching their message to the very people who had sought to crush them."

That remarkable exchange from fear to faith, from disillusionment to certainty, from hopelessness to purpose is the clear result of the Resurrection. That result is obvious in Luke's account of the Resurrection. Two discouraged disciples on the Emmaus Road were walking toward the sunset. They had accepted the finality of the Cross. Notice the wistful, bewildered regret in their words: **"We had hoped that he was the one who would redeem Israel."** (Luke 24:21)

Then Jesus joined them on their journey, but they did not recognize their Lord. He asked them about their conversation, and as the Bible says, **"They stood still, looking sad."** (Luke 24:17) Doesn't that remind you of life—ordinary life for so many people? They do not recognize Jesus, they do not accomplish anything, and their one emotion is disappointment. They just stand still and look sad.

When the disciples drew near their village, middle-eastern courtesy required that they offer Jesus hospitality for the evening. Then following an ordinary meal in an ordinary home, He took the bread, and blessed it and broke it, and gave it to them . . . just as He had done at their last supper together. And at that point, their eyes were opened, and they recognized the risen Lord, whereupon He disappeared from their sight.

When Jesus had gone from them, they hurried straight back to Jerusalem to tell the other disciples. They did not stand still, and they did not look sad. They were never again idle and purposeless. They found the other disciples and they shouted: "**The Lord is risen**", and to their amazement the others answered, "**The Lord has risen indeed . . .**" (Luke 24:34) That Easter greeting is used around the world on this glad morn. Eastern Europeans, particularly, greet each other saying "Christ is risen" and comes the reply, "He is risen, indeed".

When those disciples from the Emmaus Road first used that Resurrection greeting, the answer came back, "**He is risen indeed and appeared to Simon.**" That has to be one of the most fascinating, untold stories in the world—Simon Peter meeting with his risen Lord so soon after he had denied Him and then had wept bitterly. It must have been the intention of Jesus to comfort Peter and strengthen him for the work he was to do. He told Peter once, "**When you have turned, strengthen the brethren.**" What a turning it must have been for Peter to see the risen Lord!

Paul says, in 1st Corinthians, (15:5) that Jesus appeared to Peter first of all, but there is no record of that conversation. It may have been too dramatic for words. Sometimes the greatest understanding and the deepest truth come to us without words. We can only guess what Jesus said to Peter, or what the shame-faced apostle felt or stammered out to his Lord at their first meeting since Peter denied Him. Their reunion must have been filled with Peter's remorse and Jesus' forgiveness. That reunion must have been so richly beautiful that later, when Jesus appeared to the disciples by the Sea of Tiberius, Peter had been restored, and he was given the responsibility to care for the flock of Christ. Jesus said, "**Peter, do you love me?**" Peter answered, "**You know I love you!**" He said, "**Feed my sheep.**" (John 21:17)

Peter's greatest need was to find forgiveness and to be restored as a disciple; it was a need to be saved from self-reproach and crippling despair. The Master's pardon must have been warm, convincing and complete, because Peter, who was erratic and undependable before the Resurrection, became known after the Resurrection as "The Rock," the leader of the disciples, whose earlier confession of faith at Caesarea Philippi, "**You are the Christ, the Son of the living God.**" (Matt.16:16) became the foundation of the Church.

There is another startling account in that early Corinthian record (I Cor. 15:7), which says simply: "**Then he appeared to James.**" It is another appearance we would give anything to have witnessed, and there is no record of it. What wonder, grace, and power the scripture veils inside those simple words, "**He appeared to James.**" We are told no more than that! James was a younger brother of Jesus, one of the children Jesus, the elder brother, provided for and reared, along with Mary, their mother, after the death of Joseph. James must have worked in the carpenter's shop with Jesus, just as Jesus had worked with Joseph.

Notice, that before the Crucifixion, none of the Master's family was found among the twelve. John (7:5) said it plainly, "**The brothers of Jesus did not believe him.**" The family seemed to think He was deranged. They tried once to disrupt His public ministry and take Him home to save Him from Himself. At best they did not understand. Mary, of course, supported Him until the end, and was a witness at the Cross, but James was not there. Yet, after the Resurrection, Jesus appeared to James, and James became the prominent leader of the early Christian church in Jerusalem. Paul calls him an apostle.

What a shock the appearance of Jesus must have been to James, the Lord's brother. Like scales dropping from his eyes. He had been too close to understand. Jesus must have been completely patient with his confusion. He must have allowed him time to reflect, to put it all together, to gain the wisdom that would let him view his earthly brother as the King of Kings and the Lord of Lords. Have you noticed how the scripture underplays the emotional impact of an event? It is really astounding, but it says simply "**Then he appeared to James.**"

Saint Paul was not one of the original disciples, but Jesus appeared to him on the Damascus Road. Paul said, "**Last of all, as to one untimely born, he appeared also unto me.**" (I Corinthians 15:8) There is no evidence that Paul ever met Jesus or heard Him preach. There was only the record of his opposition: "**I persecuted the church of God . . . violently, and tried to destroy it.**" (Galatians 1:13) Oh, the power of that Damascus Road experience, where the risen Lord appeared to Paul, and turned his life around, and gave him a new cause and a new direction!

And ever since that first greeting on that first Easter, there have been Christians who have come to know "**the Lord is risen**," because He has appeared to them, "**as born out of due time**" and turned their lives around and made His home in their hearts.

> He lives! He lives! Salvation to impart,
> You ask me how I know he lives,
> He lives within my heart. [2]

That personal knowledge of the living Lord is the exciting relevancy about the Christian faith that Easter underlines. I remember hearing about a little girl, five years old, who had learned to sing, "Jesus loves me, this I know . . ." Someone asked her, "Do you really think that Jesus loves you?" She giggled her answer, "He doesn't even know me." But as she grows in years and grows in grace, she may be able to say, "**He has risen indeed**, and appeared unto me!"

In the providence of God, time is irrelevant. Jesus lives in two dimensions. As the earthly Jesus, His words and deeds are remembered and brought into the present; as the risen Christ, He is personally present and leads us into the future.

The memory of Jesus is tremendously important. As He said at the Last Supper, "**Do this in remembrance of me**." Bring the earthly Jesus forward into your current experience. Let Him influence your attitude and your behavior. The New Testament itself is the record of Jesus as remembered by the apostles. They followed the earthly Jesus, and they were witnesses to the Resurrection. They saw the risen Christ! That is what we call the apostolic faith. It is faith based on the eye-witness reports of the apostles.

Now it is critical that we know what Jesus said, what He did, how He treated people, how He felt about various things. That written record becomes our authority for Christian behavior, Christian action, and the Christian life. But memories alone lack the power to change our lives. A. E. Taylor was right, "One may fairly doubt whether . . . any man has ever really been converted to Christian faith simply by the impression made on him either by the story of Christ's life or by the reports of his moral teaching." It is the presence of Christ that brings the power. "**He is risen, indeed**, and has appeared to me."

Christ present is the power that brought the Church into existence; Christ is gloriously present with us today. Nine hundred million people praise Him in every language known to man. "**Christ is risen indeed.**"

One of the great tributes to Jesus came from Sholem Asch, a Polish Jew and Yiddish author, who wrote *The Nazarene, The Apostle, and One Destiny.* He said of Jesus: "He, as no one else before him, raised our world from the void and nothingness in which it kept losing its way. He, as no other, raised man from his probationary state as a beast, from his dumb, blind, and senseless existence—and made him part of the divine. He, as no other, works in human consciousness, like a second, higher nature . . . wakes man, calls him, raises him, and inspires him to the noblest deeds and sacrifices.

"Many of us who for one reason or another, are unable to believe in his physical resurrection . . . must never the less admit . . . that in a moral and spiritual sense the Nazarene rises from the dead every day, every hour, every minute in the hearts of millions of his believers."[3]

The power of Christ is underplayed in life just as it was underplayed in scripture. Without eyes to see you may not witness the manner of His appearing. Without faith, simple acts of charity, moments of grace, pass you by unheralded and unnoticed. Bishop Arthur Moore told about something simple that happened in a little Georgia church. A girl had fallen in love and married a man who had come into the community, and in due time they were expecting a child. Suddenly the girl's world disintegrated. Her husband left, confessing that he had left a wife and family elsewhere. Finally the baby was born, and the young mother was determined to have the child baptized in the little country church. It was a difficult moment, but when she came forward with her child, otherwise alone, twelve stewards of the church, like the twelve apostles, stood with her; they surrounded mother and child, sharing the vows to nurture the child in the faith of the Risen Lord. In so many acts of charity and kindness, Jesus the Christ is powerfully present in our actions of compassion and love. "**The Lord is risen, indeed.**"

One other thing: We are all mortal. Life does not last. It has been twenty years since I preached an Easter sermon here. Twenty years from now, I won't be back. But, we believe that the powerful God who created us, will also resurrect us, just as He did Jesus. The Master said, "**Because I live, you shall live also.**"

We don't know the nature of our resurrection, any more than we understand the Resurrection of Jesus, but we know it is a fact certain for those who love Him. Death does not end the possibility of life. It is like Carl Michalson suggested: in Christ our lives follow the pattern of a Broadway player whose role calls for his death in the first act. The curtain falls, his part is finished. All of us are actors who seem fated to die before the play is finished. As soon as the curtain falls, however, the actor leaps to his feet and dashes across the street to another theater where he takes another part. So we die to rise again! Our destiny is not explained by one stage only.

The doctrine of the Resurrection doesn't tell us the nature of the transition from one theater to another, or how long it takes; neither does it describe the scenery in the new theater. But in Christ, we know that death is not the end, we play our lives upon another stage.[4] "**Christ is risen; He is risen, indeed!**"

Oh, one more time: "**Christ is risen . . .**"

In the name of Christ, *Amen*.

Notes

1   Buechner, Frederick, *The Magnificent Defeat*, Harper & Row, 1966, p. 80.
2   Ackley, Alfred H., 1933.
3   Asch, Sholem, *One Destiny: An Epistle to the Christians*, G. P. Putnam's Sons, 1945, pg. 2.
4   Michalson, Carl, *Faith for Personal Crises*, Charles Scribner's Sons, 1958, p. 178.

19.

A Charge for 2000 and Beyond

In December of 1998, Episcopal Bishop Charles F. Duvall and Roman Catholic Archbishop Oscar H. Lipscomb agreed to lead their people in a common service of worship at the beginning of the third millennium of Jesus Christ. They also agreed to invite all other Christians in the greater Mobile area to join the celebration and participate in its planning. The date of Sunday, January 23, 2000, was chosen because it fell within the Week of Prayer for Christian Unity, and the location was the Mobile Civic Center.

The response of many Christian leaders in Mobile was both positive and enthusiastic. In the spring of 1999, a steering committee was formed with some thirty members, lay and clerical, men and women, of different races and faiths, to plan Celebration 2000.

There was much to do, and several committees were formed to accomplish the work. The committees and their chairs were: Arrangements: Very Rev. Warren Wall and Hon. Fred Richardson; Children's Participation, Ms. Candy Spitzer; Church Relations: Rev. Wesley James and Rev. Clinton Johnson; Education and Interfaith: Dr. Donald Berry and Rev. Christopher Viscardi, S. J.; Finance: Mr. John Hope, III; History: Dr. Michael Thomason; Public Relations: Mr. Bernard A. Fogarty; 2000 and Beyond: Rev. Julian Walthall and Rev. Dr. James Walters; Agape Arrangements: Ms. Jane Bledsoe and Ms. Anna Crow; Ushers: Ms. Linda Ingram; Music: Dr. Kenneth Bergdolt.

The Rev. S. Albert Kennington served not only as chairman of the Worship Committee but also as secretary to the Steering Committee. I was honored to serve as chairman of the Steering Committee. In addition to these, a much larger number of Christians, lay and clergy, from many denominations gave their time and talent to the planning and conduct of Celebration 2000.

Four thousand people attended the celebration, and the service itself was inspirational! The Rev. Warren Wall was sensitive enough to cover the altar with a beautifully embroidered frontal made by the Carmelites nuns and then placed on the center of the altar a large, open King James Bible. There were great hymns and congregational singing led by Mr. Ed Keyes and accompanied by Mr. Clinton Doolittle, organist, and Mr. Robert Holm, pianist. A combined choir of Mobile churches preformed Craig Courtney's "One Faith, One Hope, One Lord" under the direction of Dr. Sandra Willetts. While "Mobile's Singing Children" sang "Jesus Loves Me," the Civic Center was filled with "The Angels of Praise," artistically signing the words. Ms. Yvonne Madison at the piano led four thousand voices singing "Precious Lord, Take My Hand." Ms. Linda Zoghby sang "The Prayer of Saint Francis," and Mr. Chauncey Packer sang "The Lord's Prayer." Scripture was read responsively and in unison from all four gospels, the epistles of Saint Paul, Revelation, and the Old Testament. Prayers were recited from the ancient liturgy of Saint John Chrysostom, from John Wesley, and from the *Artoklasia* Service of the Greek Orthodox Church. There was a Prayer of Repentance: "We confess to you that we are sinners, and that both as individuals and as the community of your followers, we have often done what we should not have done and left undone what we should have done."

When the offering was presented, more than forty representatives of Christian ministries in Mobile—schools and colleges, agencies for rehabilitation and recovery and for homelessness and hunger, conference and retreat centers, hospitals and health care providers—placed on the altar a symbol of their ministry.

For instance, the president of the University of Mobile placed his Presidential Medallion on the altar, while the sisters of Visitation Monastery brought a box of their fund-raising Heavenly Hash and offered it to the Almighty. The entire cost of Celebration 2000 was underwritten by the J. L. Bedsole Foundation so that the total offering could be divided between The Ozanam Charitable Pharmacy of Mobile and Food for the Poor Hospital/Clinic in Port-au-Prince, Haiti.

Bread was passed along to the crowd as the people took part in a Lovefeast or *Agape* meal. The Lovefeast originated with the meals Jesus shared with His friends and in the common meals observed by the first-century Church: It was practiced in the early Church either apart from the Lord's Supper or attached to the sacrament. The Lovefeast was revived by the Moravians of Germany in the early eighteenth century and was passed on by the Wesleyan tradition. For Celebration

2000, the Lovefeast was a shared witness that all Christians are sustained by the blessings and the grace of God. In partaking of the bread, we were united in the assurance that Jesus Christ was the true bread that came down from heaven, making possible a life of eternal quality and duration.

Even though there were well over forty individuals directly involved in conducting the service, it moved smartly within the exact timeframe allotted. There were four speakers, each with a brief message: Bishop Charles F. Duval, Archbishop Oscar H. Lipscomb, Rev. Dr. Wesley A. James, and I. My remarks were entitled "A Charge for 2000 and Beyond":

> *When he had gone out, Jesus said, "Now the Son of Man has been glorified, and God has been glorified in him. If God has been glorified in him, God will also glorify him in himself and will glorify him at once. Little children, I am with you only a little longer. You will look for me; and as I said to the Jews so now I say to you, 'Where I am going, you cannot come.' I give you a new commandment, that you love one another. Just as I have loved you, you also should love one another. By this everyone will know that you are my disciples, if you have love for one another."*
>
> JOHN 13:31–35 (NRSV)

WHAT A GLORIOUS CELEBRATION! Today we celebrate two thousand years of love and grace! The love of Christ is so comprehensive that praise is more right and proper when we lift Him up together. Just look at our diversity, our differences in race, culture, and tradition! It is remarkable! We represent two thousand years of divergence and change, and yet we are one in Christ.

The traditions and cultures gathered here today contain, in our combined heritage, a glorious record of the mighty acts God has done through Jesus Christ. Across two thousand years of history, God's amazing grace in Christ has led His followers into praise, prayer, and proclamation, thanksgiving and worship, conversion and confirmation, art, architecture, and music, faith and sacrifice, education and evangelism, charity and service, and the salvation of souls. That one decisive birth has changed the world!

The history of Christianity has not been perfect. It contains too many examples of a malicious and unforgiving spirit more suitable to paganism than to Christ. Forgive us, O God, for those times when we Christians have been less than Christ-like, and do not let our sin and weakness detract from the perfection of Your glorious Son.

When the first millennium began, God prepared a time and God prepared a people, and at that time and through that people God did the unimaginable thing. The Word was made flesh. Now here we are, at the beginning of the third millennium. In His own wisdom, God has positioned us here, at this time, in this place, and with this people.

We have no idea what the future holds, whether or not it will be filled with "many dangers, toils and snares." Nor can we imagine what great things Christ has in store for those who love Him! But in any event, our calling is to follow Christ, to lift Him up, to be faithful and obedient, and to witness to God's love. Remember how the Lord Christ gave us a new commandment: **"A new commandment I give you, that you love one another."** He said: **"By this all men will know that you are my disciples, that you love one another."** (John 13:34–35)

One significant way we can witness to Christ and show the world that we are His disciples is to be obedient to His command. Let us love one another! Today, just by coming together in Christian love, we have again broken down the barriers of race, culture, and tradition, so that we are one in Christ. Here and now we are publicly proclaiming we are His disciples, that we love one another!

Celebration 2000 cannot end today—must not end today. This is only the beginning. Jesus Christ is yesterday, today and forever! I would urge all of us to continue this beginning by being deliberately inclusive, and to celebrate the third millennium by inviting other Christians into our circles of prayer and praise and Bible study, so that *everyone will know we belong to Christ.*

Let our celebration of the third millennium continue by crossing the lines of denomination and race in worship. Create opportunities to hear other Christians teach and preach and pray and sing. Share the rich diversity of Christian fellowship with one another, so that *everyone will know we belong to Christ.*

Let the celebration continue with our theologians and scholars, our schools and universities, speaking truth in love, unveiling together the height and depth and length and breadth of Christian divinity, so that *everyone will know we belong to Christ.*

Let the celebration continue by joint planning and coordinated efforts, in order that health and compassion may more effectively reach this sick and troubled world, and *everyone will know we belong to Christ.*

Finally, let our celebration of the third Christian millennium continue as we joyfully take upon ourselves the yoke of obedience, and, for love of Christ, love one another, until *everyone shall know we belong to Christ,* and every knee shall bow and every tongue confess that Jesus Christ is Lord, to the glory of God the Father!

In the name of Christ, *Amen.*

20.

Christ In You, the Hope of Glory

On Sunday, January 6, 2013, Dauphin Way United Methodist Church inaugurated its centennial year, and it was especially meaningful to me to be asked to preach on that occasion. Though I was reared in Government Street United Methodist Church, in Mobile, Alabama, and was licensed to preach from that congregation, Dauphin Way was also influential as I began my faith journey. Dr. A. Carl Adkins, pastor of Dauphin Way from 1941 until his death in 1966, was a mentor when I was in high school and during my early ministry; Carl and his family became my dear friends. During my first pastoral appointment, I was asked to speak at a Dauphin Way youth retreat conducted by the legendary James Mason who was Director of Youth Ministry. (Later, Jim served on the staff while I was senior minister at Dauphin Way.) As a young minister, twenty-six years old, I was invited to read the scripture for one of the opening services celebrating Dauphin Way's new sanctuary. (G. Bromley Oxnam, bishop of the Washington Episcopal Area, was the preacher on that occasion.) In 1966, Dr. Joel D. McDavid and I traveled together to Dauphin Way for the funeral of Dr. Adkins, neither of us aware that we both would follow Carl as pastors of this great church.

The centennial year at Dauphin Way has already been rich and fulfilling. Under the guidance of Mrs. Kimi Oaks, chairperson of the Centennial Steering Committee, several hundred members have worked to design special events and exhibits, to plan educational and worship opportunities, and to reach out to former members, staff, clergy and those who have entered into Christian service from Dauphin Way.

I felt the opening service of the centennial year should honor those heroes of the past and review the history of the church, but more importantly it should redefine the church as the Body of Christ and focus on the next centennial of faithful witness and service; so I preached from the words of Paul in Colossians, "Christ in you, the hope of glory":

> *I became its [the church's] servant according to God's commission that was given to me for you, to make the word of God fully known, the mystery that has been hidden throughout the ages and generations but has now been revealed to his saints. To them God chose to make known how great among the Gentiles are the riches of the glory of this mystery, which is Christ in you . . . the hope of glory.*
>
> COLOSSIANS 1:26–27 (NRSV)

> *Christ in you . . . the hope of all the glorious things to come.*
>
> COLOSSIANS 1:27 (J. B. PHILLIPS)

TODAY, AS A CONGREGATION, we are entering into a year of centennial celebration. During this year we will review the history of this church. We will ask how it began; who were its leaders both lay and clerical; what have been its signal accomplishments; where lay its pitfalls and dangers; who were the strong saints of the church; who entered the ministry of the wider church from this congregation; where are we now and what can we expect in the future? All these things and more will be considered, remembered, studied, and catalogued because on January 5, 2014—one year from to-day—Dauphin Way United Methodist Church will have been in existence one hundred years.

Only this year of all years, only you and I of all people will have the opportunity to prepare for and experience the Dauphin Way centennial. This should be a year of reflection and turning to the Lord, a year when we determine how to claim the future and manage God's many gifts of grace, a "year of jubilee."

In ancient Israel the trumpet sound of the ram's horn on the Day of Atonement announced a year of jubilee. The jubilee year occurred every fifty years at the end of "seven weeks of years." That jubilee year began with prayer and fasting and the forgiveness of sins, and became a year of freedom and celebration. **"And you shall hallow the fiftieth year and you shall proclaim liberty throughout the land to all its inhabitants."** (Leviticus 25:10) Jubilee was a year of emancipation: the fields lay fallow; all property was returned to its ancestral owners; defaulting debtors and Israelite slaves were all set free. The rationale for all this was simply that the land belonged to God and could not be sold absolutely; the Israelites were the children of God and could not be enslaved perpetually.

There is no evidence that the law of jubilee was ever applied. It was an ideal of justice and social equality that was never realized. Jubilee was a utopian dream, but it was a strong reminder that we are stewards in this earthly existence; we are managers not owners. Everything we possess belongs to God: our time, talent, and our treasure. All we accomplish is completed at His pleasure, civilization and order, the arts and literature, the sciences and services.

A jubilee year at Dauphin Way would signal that God is watching us with unrelenting interest! He is watching not only our national politics and personal life but certainly our Christian life, and without a doubt, He watches our church! You can be sure that throughout the past, present and future, what we have done as a congregation, what we do now, and how we shape the future are all of singular concern to God the Father. "His eye is on the sparrow, and I know He watches me."[1]

God is always watching! It was true from the beginning. In Genesis (16:7–13) when Hagar, the mother of Ishmael, fled from her mistress Sarai, the angel of the Lord found her in the wilderness and promised to so greatly multiply her descendants that they could "not be numbered for multitude." Then Hagar called the name of the Lord who spoke to her "You-Are-the-God-Who-Sees" or "Thou, God, seest me."

Clearly God is watching *us*, so we need to hear the story of a little boy who visited his grandmother in the retirement home. During the visit the boy kept looking at a picture on the wall. It was the all-seeing eye of God and underneath was that quotation from Genesis (16:13) "Thou, God, seest me." Grandmother said, "Do you know what that means?" The boy said, "Yes ma'am, it means God is watching to see everything I do wrong."

"Oh no," said grandmother. "It means God loves you so much, He cannot take His eyes off you."[2]

Remember, in spite of all we do, while at our best or our worst, God loves us unconditionally. In response to that great love I pray that this centennial anniversary will be a Jubilee Year, a time when we as faithful and devoted stewards return all we have and all we are to our gracious redeeming God.

How can we accomplish this impossible task? How can we become more like the Master? How can we go on toward perfection? How can we do the work of Christ? In our own feeble powers we cannot even achieve what we intend to achieve. We are like Paul, **"For I do not do what I want, but I do the very thing I hate."** (Rom. 7:15) Yet there is an answer! In his letter to the Colossian church, Paul had a *jubilee insight*. He explained his unique calling which was to share the good news of Christ with everyone, Jew and gentile alike, and claimed his commission which was **"to announce the secret hidden for long ages."** (1:26)

And what a glorious secret it is! That uncovered secret is the good news of the gospel: the love and mercy of God are offered to all people beyond the limits of race, nationality, age, or gender. That was Paul's jubilee insight; that all hope of salvation, all desire for justice and righteousness can actually be accomplished by the indwelling of Christ. That's the open secret; that's how everything is accomplished; that's how God's Kingdom comes. The secret is **"Christ in you . . . the hope of all the glorious things to come."** (Col. 1:27, J. B. Phillips) Let this line from Colossians be the theme of our centennial year—**"Christ in you . . . the hope of all the glorious things to come."**

Paul was in a Roman prison when he wrote those words to the church at Colossae. Colossae was never an important city; it was "the most unimportant town to which Paul ever wrote a letter."[3] We only know the name of one member of the church at Colossae, Epaphras, and we know him because he left Colossae and traveled with Paul. Even the site is unspectacular and disappointing. Little remains above ground. All that the modern traveler sees is simply a huge mound, a *tell*, under which is buried the ancient city.[4]

And yet, in that letter to such an unimportant place, Paul wrote the highest reaches of his thought.[5] He spoke of Christ unforgettably as the **"visible image of the invisible God,"** and that letter kept the Christian faith pure from the Gnostic heresies and clarified the vision of the generations after. Paul said that this is the amazing mystery of the Incarnation: "**Christ in you . . . the hope of all the glorious things to come.**"

Like Colossae, Dauphin Way may not be a notable church by historic standards or numerical strength, but it can look back upon many glorious moments and significant accomplishments. In the past ninety-nine years well over nineteen thousand persons have entered into membership at Dauphin Way and, incidentally, there never was any practice of segregation, shutting anyone out. The church is more diverse than it was in 1914 racially, geographically, nationally, socially. It is no longer a neighborhood church, but a church offering Christ in many different ways, to more people than our own, to more countries than our own. We are a part of the Church Universal; our service ministry and missionary outreach have spread to Peru, Jamaica, Mexico, Costa Rica, Belize, Nigeria, and Cameroon. Who can measure the influence, the salvation, the evangelism, the healing, the reconciliation, the service, the love that has flowed through the life-pulse—the "incarnation"—of this congregation?

Like Colossae our beginning was inglorious. Dauphin Way began with twenty children in Sunday School a hundred years ago in the summer of 1913. As Sunday School increased, an old saw mill shed was dismantled and moved to the corner of Dauphin and Houston Streets. From that beginning the church was formed, and the membership grew and the buildings multiplied, and the mission increased. Many of its own sons and daughters have entered into Christian ministry, and of no less importance are those who have become Christian parents or dedicated doctors, lawyers, judges, teachers, nurses, business leaders, architects, scientists, and builders, citizens of the City of God.

Christopher Morley was very observant when he said:

> Never write up your diary
> On the day itself:
> It takes longer than that
> To know what happened.

That was true of every great day in history. It was true of the day Martin Luther nailed his theses on the door of Wittenburg Castle. It was true of a little prayer meeting in Aldersgate Street in London. It was especially true of Good Friday, and it was true of a Sunday School meeting at 1770 Dauphin Street in the summer of 1913. God's kingdom grows quietly, silently, unexpectedly. It grows from small, inauspicious beginnings and accomplishes remarkable feats under the mysterious guidance of Almighty God.

A centennial observation is a backward glance and that reflection is important because "We live forward, we understand backward."[6] It would be tragic for our church to have a hundred years of experience and miss the meaning. Looking back, we can acknowledge the accomplishments, but let me remind you that with deeper dedication, more willing sacrifice, more regard for Christ and less regard for self or even for the church, we could have, we should have done greater things in His name.

Christianity has no laurels to rest upon. The Christian faith is only one generation away from extinction and certainly cannot use any past achievement as an excuse for idleness. Remembering our stained-glass window, a child once described a saint as "a person the light shines through." But I tell you, if these transparent saints, these stained-glass pillars of the church, could step out of the window, they would not talk about the victories they had won. They would say, Let's get on with the work of offering salvation, of proclaiming the good news, of serving the poor, and glorifying the mighty God.

When that great chancel window was installed at Dauphin Way, three persons pictured there were still alive. It is always dangerous to name your saints too early. But technically, our church does not name its saints at all. We know, of course, in the life of the local church, those exemplary Christians who have honored Christ with a life of love and service. But we also know there are a multitude of unknown saints, equally devoted to Christ, whose faithfulness cannot be honored because their victory is anonymous.

Gregory Bateson, the English anthropologist, tells about New College in Oxford, England. The main hall was built in the 1600s with beams forty feet long and two feet thick. Recently, a committee was formed to find replacement trees because the beams were suffering from dry rot. They found the replacement cost prohibitive and there were no mature English forests with forty-foot oaks. A young faculty member suggested they ask the college forester, because over the years certain lands had been given to the college. When they brought in the forester, he said, "We've been wondering when you would ask. When the building was constructed 350 years ago, the architects specified that a grove of trees be planted and maintained to replace the beams in the ceiling when they would suffer from dry rot."[7]

That made me think of the pillars of the church, the great and sturdy oaks whose strength and wisdom sustained this congregation throughout the century past. What is being done to replace those fallen giants? None of the thirty-seven charter members are still alive. The last one, Ms. Lillian Culpepper McGowin, died twenty-one years ago, in 1992. Most of us won't be here in one hundred years, but whether or not this outpost of God's holy Church will be alive and well in a hundred years will be determined in the meantime by one thing: "**Christ in you . . . the hope of all the glorious things to come.**"

So, what of the future? How can we win the future for Christ? There is only one way, "**Christ in you . . . the hope of all the glorious things to come!**" Here is the question for today. Where should the church focus its priorities in the new centennial?

There is only one answer. In the new centennial the church should carefully focus its priorities on following and trusting the Spirit of Christ. We Methodists spend a lot of energy tinkering with the organization, shaping the structures of the church. That alone is an inadequate response to the multi-cultural secularism and religious fanaticism of our time. The primary question is how should we conduct our worship, design our work, and shape our mission in complete harmony with the Spirit of Christ? Nothing less will satisfy the satiated emptiness of our time.

In the 1830s, after Ralph Waldo Emerson lost his wife, he traveled to Europe seeking some recovery. He went over on a sailing ship and returned on a steamship. He remarked on his return voyage that he missed the "Aeolian connection."[8] In Greek mythology, Aeolus was the son of Poseidon and the Keeper of the Winds. Traveling home on a noisy steamship, spilling oil on the water and smoke in the sky, Emerson missed the quiet naturalness of the sun and the wind and the open air. You know, of course, that in Hebrew the word for *wind*, *breath*, and *spirit* are all the same. In our busy, clamorous, technological world we need to be sure of an "Aeolian connection," a connection with the Spirit of Christ, the Breath of God. The congregation, no less than the individual, must be led by the Spirit of the Lord. **"Christ in you . . . the hope of all the glorious things to come."**

Only Christ, incarnate in His followers, will claim the future. I don't mean to be pessimistic, but looking back across one hundred years we know that life is mortal, and time is continuous; "the generations rise and pass away." This day, which the Lord has made, is unique; it is never to be repeated. There will be only one January 6, 2013, and yet this unique, unrepeatable and irreplaceable day must come to an end. It will leave at its appointed time to make place for tomorrow. Creativity understands this. Thomas Mann said, "Without death there would scarcely have been poets on earth."[9] Michelangelo said, "No thought exists in me which death has not carved with his chisel."[10] The passage of time is relentless and death is inevitable, but death itself can be positive and creative whenever we honor the urge to leave something of importance, something of value, to those who follow.

Watching over this congregation through these many years, I have been amazed at those individuals who are touched by the Spirit of Christ. They emerge out of obscurity; they are gifted beyond any expectation; they break the barriers of tradition and culture; they reach new heights of sacrifice and service. They are just ordinary people, like you and me, but they are incarnated with the Spirit of Christ. We have learned from them, received our faith and hope from them, and, in the same way, it will be our belief and dedication, yours and mine, shaped by our commitment and individuality that will be handed on to another generation.

Alexander Irvine wrote a classic Irish story about a group of neighbors who live in County Antrim, Ireland. He called it "My Lady of the Chimney Corner," and said it was "a true story at the bottom of the world." Published in 1913, one hundred years ago, it describes the peasant life of Anna Gilmore, who is prominent in the story, but not prominent in the town or in the church. Most of the village people would not know her. She didn't seek obscurity, it just seemed to find her, and find her often seated in her chimney corner.

On one occasion, a young fisherman named Henry Luckie died suddenly, and Eliza, his mother, came at once in search of Anna. Anna was the angel of God to her friends. She took charge of the arrangements and she talked to Eliza about death as a partnership gone broke between the body and the soul, and how Eliza needed the spirit of God. Anna said God comes to you in many ways, but you will have to be calm before He comes. Eliza said finally, "I am at peace now." So Anna said, "Well, get down on your knees and talk with Him, tell Him about your empty home and your sore heart." So Eliza did just that. Anna said, "Ask Him to lay His hand on your tired head in token that He is with you in your distress. Then, after a moment, "as gently as falls an autumn leaf," Anna laid her hand on Eliza's head. "Oh, Oh, Oh!" cried Eliza. "He's done it. Glory to God, He's done it!" She said, "It was so nice, it felt like your hand, Anna." Anna said, "It was my hand, but it was God's hand, too."

Then she said, "Listen dear, God's arm is not shortened. God takes a hand wherever He can find it, and just does what He likes with it. Sometimes He takes a bishop's hand and lays it on a child's head in benediction; then He takes the hand of a doctor to relieve pain, and the hand of a mother to guide her child; and sometimes He takes the hand of an old creature like me to give a bit of comfort to a neighbor. But they are all hands touched by His spirit, and His spirit is everywhere looking for hands to use."[11]

That can happen in this jubilee year and in the next centennial. God can use our hands, God can use our hearts, and He will use them, here in our church, here in our time. But it can only happen with **"Christ in you . . . in *you* . . . the hope of all the glorious things to come."**

In the name of Christ, *Amen.*

NOTES

1   "His Eye Is on the Sparrow," Civilla D. Martin, 1905.

2   "Because God Loves You: A Message from U. S. Catholic Bishops for the Jubilee Year 2000," p. 3.

3   Barclay, William, *The Letters to The Philippians, Colossians, and Thessalonians,* Westminster Press, 1957, p.113.

4   Trainor, Father Michael, Flinders University, Australia, at.

5   Barclay, William, op. cit., p.122.

6   James, William.

7   McDonough, William, "A Centennial Sermon: Design, Ecology, Ethics and the Making of Things," delivered at The Cathedral of St. John the Divine, N. Y., 1993.

8   Ibid.

9   Kubler-Ross, *Elizabeth, Death, the Final Stage of Growth*, Simon & Schuster, Inc., 1975, p. 2.

10   Ibid.

11   Irvine, Alexander, *My Lady of the Chimney Corner*, The Century Company, 1913, p. 96.

Acknowledgments

I am indebted to the people of many congregations who have loved and listened and borne with me, but none more than Dauphin Way United Methodist Church. Through nearly four decades they have been a people who offered me their friendship and joined me in expressing faith and loyalty to Christ; they gave me the freedom to witness as I was called and to serve where I could. "What wondrous love is this . . ."

I am deeply grateful to Frye Gaillard for his patience and quiet insistence that this work might possibly be accomplished—and more importantly, that perhaps it should be accomplished.

When I retired, Mrs. Elizabeth Patton volunteered to help organize my sermons. She worked at length to transcribe the material, creating a database of title, text, and occasion so that I might recover the material as needed. The assistance has been invaluable.

I am not original and it worried me that memory was unreliable and I could not always credit the sources of my thought. An article by Dr. Oliver Sacks on source confusions of memory reassured me that I was not alone. He noted that Mark Twain wrote to Helen Keller when she was accused of plagiarism, ". . . all ideas are second-hand, consciously or unconsciously, drawn from a million outside sources."[1]

NOTES

1   Sacks, Oliver, *The New York Review of Books*, February 21, 2013, Speak, Memory, p. 19.

About the Author

Stephen F. Dill is retired after forty years of service as a United Methodist minister. He is pastor emeritus of Dauphin Way United Methodist Church in Mobile, Alabama, and director emeritus of the J. L. Bedsole Scholars Program. He holds BA and MA degrees from Emory University and in 1975 was awarded an honorary doctorate by Huntingdon College in Montgomery, Alabama.